Sacred Borders and
East Lothian

SACRED PLACES SERIES

Sacred Borders and East Lothian

SCOTLAND'S CHURCHES SCHEME

SAINT ANDREW PRESS
Edinburgh

First published in 2010 by
SAINT ANDREW PRESS
121 George Street
Edinburgh EH2 4YN

ISBN 978 0 7152 0945 5

British Library Cataloguing in Publication Data
A catalogue record for this book is available from the British Library.

It is the publisher's policy to only use papers that are natural and recyclable and that
have been manufactured from timber grown in renewable, properly managed forests.
All of the manufacturing processes of the papers are expected to conform to the
environmental regulations of the country of origin.

Typeset in Enigma by Waverley Typesetters, Warham, Norfolk
Manufactured in Great Britain by Bell & Bain Ltd, Glasgow

BUCKINGHAM PALACE

As Patron of Scotland's Churches Scheme, I warmly welcome this publication as part of the *Sacred Places* series of books being produced by the Scheme.

The story of the heritage and culture of Scotland would be lacking significantly without a strong focus on its churches and sacred sites. I am sure that this guidebook will be a source of information and enjoyment both to the people of Scotland and to our visitors.

Anne

Scotland's Churches Scheme

www.sacredscotland.org.uk

Scotland's Churches Scheme is an ecumenical charitable trust, providing an opportunity to access the nation's living heritage of faith by assisting the 'living' churches in membership to:

- Promote spiritual understanding by enabling the public to appreciate all buildings designed for worship and active as living churches
- Work together with others to make the Church the focus of the community
- Open their doors with a welcoming presence
- Tell the story of the building (however old or new), its purpose and heritage (artistic, architectural and historical)
- Provide information for visitors, young and old

The Scheme has grown rapidly since its inception in 1994, and there are now more than 1,200 churches in membership. These churches are spread across Scotland and across the denominations.

The *Sacred Scotland* theme promoted by Scotland's Churches Scheme focuses on the wish of both visitors and local communities to be able to access our wonderful range of church buildings in a meaningful way, whether the visit be occasioned by spiritual or heritage motivation or both. The Scheme can advise and assist member churches on visitor welcome, and, with its range of 'how-to' brochures, provide information on research, presentation, security and other live issues. The Scheme, with its network of local representatives, encourages the opening of doors and the care of tourists and locals alike, and offers specific services such as the provision of grants for organ-playing.

Sacred Scotland (www.sacredscotland.org.uk), the website of Scotland's Churches Scheme, opens the door to Scotland's story by exploring living traditions of faith in city, town, village and island across the country. The site is a portal to access information on Scotland's churches of all denominations and is a starting point for your special journeys.

We are delighted to be working with Saint Andrew Press in the publication of this series of regional guides to Scotland's churches. In 2009, the first three volumes were published – *Sacred South-West Scotland*; *Sacred Fife and the Forth Valley*; and *Sacred Edinburgh and Midlothian*. This volume, *Sacred Borders and East Lothian*, is one of three being published in 2010 (the others are *Sacred Glasgow and the Clyde Valley* and *Sacred North-East Scotland*), to be followed by a further three books in 2011, when the whole country will have been covered. We are grateful to the authors of the introductory articles, Professor John Hume, one of our trustees, and Mary Low, for their expert contributions to our understanding of sacred places.

The growth of 'spiritual tourism' worldwide is reflected in the million-plus people who visit Scotland's religious sites annually. We hope that the information in this book will be useful in bringing alive the heritage as well as the ministry of welcome which our churches offer. In the words of our former President, Lady Marion Fraser: 'we all owe a deep debt of gratitude to the many people of vision who work hard and imaginatively to create a lasting and peaceful atmosphere which you will carry away with you as a special memory when you leave'.

Dr Brian Fraser
Director
Scotland's Churches Scheme
Dunedin
Holehouse Road
Eaglesham
Glasgow
G76 0JF

Invitation to Pilgrimage

Borders and East Lothian

What is it about empty churches? Is it the light, the stillness, the strange alchemy of polish, beeswax, flowers, mould, incense and old stone? No two are the same. Some are dark and austere; others have glorious windows, kneelers and other works of art. Most have memorials of some kind, reminders of mortality, empire and the ravages of war. Many have scripture verses, carved in stone or engraved on brass. You might barely notice them, but they can catch you off guard. 'Lo, I am with you always, even unto the end of the world' can sound distinctly personal at the right moment.

At Linton, a simple notice in the porch reminds you that 'This is none other than the house of God and the gate of heaven'. You might have come to see the interesting old tympanum above the porch, or a worn carving of a knight slaying a ferocious beast or two; but the notice invites a different mood, less detached, more present. The words come from the story of Jacob in the book of Genesis. Jacob is fleeing from his brother, whom he has cheated, and is sleeping rough in a place far from home. That night, he has a vivid dream in which he sees a ladder reaching from earth to heaven. Angels are going up and down on it – and at the very top is none other than the God of his ancestors, speaking to him directly, not with accusations but with promises of help. He wakes up, trembling. The foot of the ladder had been right beside his pillow. He had not known that God could be so near, or so interested in his fate. Churches can be remarkable for their architecture and history – but step aside for a moment, lay down the guidebook, and stand or sit quietly in one of these sacred places, and you may find yourself crossing the invisible threshold between tourist and pilgrim.

Perhaps we are pilgrims by nature. There is restlessness in us, a craving for something that is hard to name and even harder to locate. Is it to be found in some quiet country church or ruined abbey, in a distant country, in front of our nose, above us, within us? If we travel, will we come closer to it? There are those who say it is right here. No need to go anywhere. 'Go and sit in your cell and your cell will teach you everything' said one of the Desert Hermits. Stay right where you are. Among the pots and pans. Glory to God in the High Street. But the restlessness remains and is often assuaged by travelling, especially walking. Thousands of years ago, the Psalmist made a song about a pilgrimage to Jerusalem and what he hoped to find there: 'As the deer longs for running streams, so do I long for you, my God'. The longing here is almost physical, like an animal instinct. Centuries later, Mary and Joseph walked the eighty miles from Nazareth to Jerusalem for the feast of the Passover, with friends and neighbours and their 12-year-old son, Jesus. In a similar way, though they would express and understand it differently, Buddhists go to Bodh Gaya, Muslims to Mecca, Hindus to Varanasi and so on. Those who cannot travel so far – or see no need to – go to local holy places. The church on the corner might do. In fact, most communities have traditional holy places where the power of God has been celebrated in nature, people or events. In medieval times, pilgrims made spiritual as well as practical preparations for the longer journeys. Some even made a will, if the road was dangerous or the natives hostile. Most brought gifts or offerings of some kind. And, although some undoubtedly went for the company, even the adventure, most carried with them some prayer or desire which was the secret – or not-so-secret – reason for their journey.

Nowadays, we might hesitate to give a reason, other than curiosity or a break from routine; but traditional pilgrimages had an unashamedly serious purpose. There would be people seeking healing or forgiveness, a good harvest, a fruitful marriage, a successful enterprise. Others came to give thanks – for the birth of a baby, a narrow escape, even victory in battle. If it had been possible to see these prayers rising to heaven like incense, the air above some of our Border abbeys would have shimmered with them. Melrose in its heyday was one of the four 'heid pilgrimages' of Scotland. A steady stream of people came to pray there, at the tomb of St Waltheof in the abbey church and at the older chapel of St Cuthbert a few miles away at Old Melrose. Saints were widely seen as friends at the court of heaven, people whose prayers, joined with those of ordinary mortals, might be particularly helpful. Who knows what schemes, what dodgy petitions were whispered at these set-apart places? But then, as now, many who came with a sincere heart found themselves changed as they spoke the words or inarticulate sounds that expressed their needs, their truest feelings.

Most pilgrimage centres also had physicians on hand; but medicine in the Middle Ages was still closely related to the 'cure of souls', so the sacraments had a role to play, as did the local community and your fellow-pilgrims. A pilgrimage could be undertaken not for your own sake but on behalf of a friend or relative. There was a great generosity in this – but, as the centuries wore on, the custom grew up of employing someone to go on pilgrimage for you, if you could afford it, thus avoiding any great hardship or disruption to your life. This sort of thing gave the Church a bad name, but it shows how real the benefits of pilgrimage were believed to be.

As for thanksgiving pilgrimages, in the 1430s, the future Pope Pius II made a pilgrimage to Whitekirk in East Lothian in fulfilment of a vow. He was almost shipwrecked on his arrival in Scotland and had sworn at the height of the storm that, if he survived, he would walk barefoot to the nearest shrine – which happened to be Whitekirk. His intention was to keep that promise, but perhaps there was something else as well. Had he found himself far from ready to meet his God on the high seas (or even just the Firth of Forth), so that his pilgrimage was also partly penitential, an acknowledgement of the gap between the person he was and the person he believed God wanted him to be? Aeneas Sylvius (as he was called then) was not a villain, as far as I know; but people who had committed serious crimes were sometimes sent on pilgrimage in the belief that it could change them for the better. This was not intended to be a soft option. The belief was that the physical demands of a long, arduous journey on foot would both punish the body and purge the soul, ready for a fresh start.

A different kind of pilgrimage existed in the Celtic tradition. There are at least two examples – one story and one historical report – of Irish monks deliberately casting away their oars and drifting in open boats, not knowing where they would end up. It was an exercise in trust and renunciation, no doubt with a dash of heroism thrown in, but it is not widely attested and was probably related to an older custom in which malefactors (rather than penitents) were cast adrift and left to the judgement of the elements. This seems to be what happened to St Theneu, mother of St Kentigern. Unjustly accused of fornication, she is cast adrift on the Forth, having survived an earlier attempt to throw her off a mountain, possibly Traprain Law near Haddington; but her prayers are answered and she is brought safely ashore at Culross, where she gives birth to a little boy.

Peregrinatio, pilgrimage, can also mean 'wandering', and this is what the Irish monks were doing – not just the reckless ones who threw away their oars, but also the far larger number who set off on open-ended journeys up the west coast of Scotland into the North Atlantic, across the Irish Sea, even to the continent. No shrine was identified, no holy place sought out. In many ways, it was the very opposite of the other pilgrimages. They set out into unknown territory, with no home comforts and no security, seeking only the 'kingdom of God', which is not so much a point on a map as a way of being. Such journeys were inspired partly by the faith of Abraham and Moses, who set out through a trackless wilderness to a promised land; but, in Luke's Gospel, Jesus says: 'Whoever would be a follower of mine must leave self behind, take up his cross daily and come, follow me'. He was heading for Jerusalem at the time, but he was describing another journey as well, one of passionate commitment to the love of God and neighbour.

The whole of life can be a pilgrimage in this sense, and the Church a pilgrim people. A little boy born in Berwickshire around 1265 followed his calling first into the Franciscan order, then into the newly unfolding world of scholastic philosophy. He became known as 'John the Scotsman from Duns', or John Duns Scotus, one of the greatest religious thinkers of the Middle Ages. During the seventeenth century, thousands of nameless people were caught up in a long struggle against absolute monarchy. The argument was often couched in religious terms, with the Covenanters refusing to accept that the king was head of the Church. For this, and for other 'treasonable' activities, men and women were imprisoned on the Bass Rock, off North Berwick, in the 1670s and 1680s. Some of them had blood on their hands, as did their opponents; but their independent spirit and love of scripture are part of Scotland's Christian heritage to this day. In the churchyard at Ettrick lie the mortal remains of James Hogg 'the Ettrick shepherd', whose 1824 novel *The Private Memoirs and Confessions of a Justified Sinner* dared to imagine a theology tested to destruction, albeit by a misguided individual. It did not make Hogg popular, but it was a work of extraordinary insight about the human capacity for self-deception. Another lifetime pilgrim was Scotland's first deaconess, Lady Grisell Baillie. She had been working with women and children for most of her life, in what we would now call community work, education and public health, when she was formally 'set apart' as a deaconess in Bowden Kirk in 1888.

It is not necessary to leave home to be a pilgrim of the mind or a lifetime pilgrim in this sense; but, if you have itchy feet, the Borders provides the perfect opportunity to work off some of your restlessness. St Cuthbert's Way runs from Melrose to Lindisfarne in Northumberland and covers about sixty miles. It is not a traditional pilgrim route, nor was it designed specifically for religious people, but it is more than just a pleasant country stroll. It crosses a landscape which Cuthbert and his contemporaries would have known back in the seventh century, before any of the sacred places in this book had been drawn or thought of. There were, of course, earlier sacred places: stone circles in the Cheviot Hills, hilltops, springs and water courses, trees; but the first Christian Britons left signs of their faith in carved stones and Latin inscriptions in the valleys around Ettrick, Yarrow and Peebles. Their churches were made of wood and have not survived. The same goes for the churches built by the Anglian settlers who abandoned Thor and Odin in the years following 634. Their leaders were the Northumbrian king, St Oswald, baptised and educated in Iona, and St Aidan, a monk from the same tradition. Cuthbert would have known these hills and rivers, the coastline, even some of the roads and paths. He would have been amazed by the scale and solidity of the Cistercian abbey which sprang up on the north side of the Eildon Hills 500 years after he was born. His own monastery was at Old Melrose a few miles away. It was an Anglo-Celtic foundation, part of the network of monasteries which looked to St Columba as their founder and patron.

St Cuthbert's Way starts in Melrose, crosses the Eildons and passes through St Boswells. This sleepy village and its more workaday neighbour, Newtown St Boswells, take their names from Boisil, Cuthbert's scripture teacher and mentor. He was also pastor to the villages round about; and Cuthbert followed in his footsteps, travelling by river or on foot, teaching, baptising and 'living among the rough hill folk' for days, sometimes weeks on end. He would have been quite familiar with Dere Street, the old Roman road which forms part of St Cuthbert's Way in places. He often walked by the Tweed. Once, somewhere on the banks of the Teviot, he came across an 'eagle' eating a large fish. A boy who was travelling with him ran forwards and grabbed the fish for their dinner, but Cuthbert insisted on giving half of it back to the eagle and sharing the remainder with some strangers whom they happened to meet. The 'eagle' was probably an osprey – and you might still see one hereabouts if you are very lucky. The hike over the Cheviots can be demanding – and exhilarating – as can the crossing to Lindisfarne, whether you take the causeway or plowter across the sand flats at low tide. The sea comes in fast here and deserves enormous respect. Like any pilgrimage, St Cuthbert's Way brings you, sooner or later, into close contact with the incontestable rhythms of nature, the weather and your own vulnerability and resourcefulness.

Today's pilgrimages are part of ancient tradition, but they are also new. There is less emphasis nowadays on the cult of saints – and rightly so, since these holy men and women never intended to be the main centres of attention. Fading too is the paralysing sense of guilt which so often prevented people from experiencing the love of God. We are less preoccupied with our eternal destiny, most of the time, and are more aware of how Jesus saw his message: as good news in this life for the poor, blind, crippled and enslaved. The natural world has become an important part of many pilgrimages, as we notice its fragility as well as its beauty. We may also find, as we travel, opportunities to practise the kind of people skills which might just allow six billion neighbours of different cultures and persuasions to live together on one small planet. But the heart of pilgrimage is the same: to come home to God, to give thanks.

Come to the Borders and East Lothian on a Sunday morning, and you will find living communities of faith gathered in buildings of varying ages and styles. Come during the week, and most of them will be empty. The Church is outside, in the people, where it belongs. But emptiness holds a space for prayer, for listening. It can be as fertile as any garden. So don't hurry away. God's way for the world is not always what, or where, we expect it to be. Too tight a schedule, too organised a route, can close down possibilities and keep us safely, too safely, within the confines of habit. Live a little. Enjoy the journey and the destination. Or stay at home and invite a friend round for a curry. Wherever you find yourself, the words of the old hymn for Holy Thursday make a good compass: 'ubi caritas et amor, Deus ibi est' – 'Where there is charity and love, God is there'.

MARY LOW
Melrose

Introduction

Sacred Borders and East Lothian

The area covered in this book is primarily rural, and much of it upland. There are many small villages, originally built to serve the agricultural parishes in which they are set. The few towns are of widely varying character. Musselburgh, North Berwick, Dunbar and Eyemouth were all ports, grain-exporting in the early nineteenth century, and then bases for fishing fleets, as were (and to some extent still are) the villages of Cockenzie and Port Seton and St Abbs. Musselburgh, with coal in its hinterland, became an industrial centre with a paper mill, a large net factory, breweries and a world-famous wire works. Also on the coast, the village of Prestonpans had, besides its salt pans, a sulphuric-acid works (the first large one in the world) and a noted brewery. Dunbar and North Berwick both became dormitory towns for Edinburgh, and holiday resorts, in the later nineteenth century. Haddington, county town of East Lothian, remains quintessentially a market town. Historically, its industries – corn-milling, distilling and, earlier, tarred woollen manufacture – were rooted in the agriculture of the area, but there are also modern industries. Duns and Kelso, county towns of Berwickshire and Roxburghshire respectively, are comparable but smaller: their administrative functions, with those of Peebles and Selkirk, have since 1975 been transferred to Newtown St Boswells, itself no more than a village.

The inland towns in the Borders are all in the river valleys, dominated by the hills of the Southern Uplands. Peebles, a wool town, became in the later nineteenth century, like

Fig. 1. The ruined Dunglass Collegiate Church, East Lothian

Fig. 2. The former Seton Collegiate Church, East Lothian

Dunbar and North Berwick, a dormitory town and resort. Innerleithen, Galashiels, Jedburgh, Selkirk and Hawick retained their domination by textile manufacture (mainly woollens) until the later twentieth century, with Hawick specialising in hosiery manufacture. Innerleithen, model for Sir Walter Scott's 'St Ronan's Well', also had a brief vogue as a spa. Melrose, with its evocative ruined abbey, was one of Scotland's first tourist towns, also popularised by Scott. It was the construction of the North British Railway's Hawick Branch and later extensions that opened up the Borders to outside influences. The railways supplied the towns with coal, visitors and raw materials for their industries and took away their fine textiles to markets in the United Kingdom and abroad.

The agriculture of the area was historically, and remains, very varied. In the heart of the Borders, sheep-farming dominated, with some arable farming in the valleys. Much of East Lothian and Berwickshire, however, became the most important grain-growing areas in Scotland. Consolidation of landholdings in the seventeenth and eighteenth centuries was followed by the introduction of improved farming techniques, notably rotation of crops, manuring and plant-breeding. The invention and speedy adoption of the threshing machine (invented by an East Lothian man, Andrew Meikle, and marketed from 1789) made large-scale grain-growing much more economic. Because of the availability of coal, many farms introduced fixed steam engines in the mid-nineteenth century to power threshing mills and other machinery such as turnip- and chaff-cutters. Much of the grain grown in the Merse of Berwickshire and in East Lothian was shipped coastwise, and there are still large grain stores in North Berwick, Dunbar and Eyemouth, now adapted to other purposes. More recently, barley has been intensively grown, historically to supply Edinburgh's massive brewing industry and its now

Fig. 3. The ruined St Martin's Church, Haddington, East Lothian

Fig. 4. Former chapel by harbour,
North Berwick, East Lothian

largely forgotten whisky-distilling industry. Barley from the area is still largely used by the Scotch whisky industry.

This economic background helps us to understand the history of the churches of the area, but it is also worth looking briefly at the political history of the area. The Borders, as the term implies, was for centuries debatable land, with frequent cross-Border skirmishes and periodic full-scale invasions – features of the largely unresolved hostility between England and Scotland. Sometimes, incursions from the south continued up into East Lothian en route to Edinburgh and the central Lowlands. The Border abbeys of Kelso, Melrose, Jedburgh and Dryburgh all suffered spectacularly during such invasions, but smaller religious establishments were not immune, and some were sacked. It is notable that Ladykirk, overlooking the Border, and Dunglass and Seton collegiate churches were all built with a minimum of combustible material. On the other hand, the scale and architectural sophistication of these and other medieval churches in the area, such as St Mary's, Haddington, is clear evidence of the prosperity of the area in the medieval and early modern period – the very prosperity that made it worth invading. The Border abbeys were apparently sustained by sheep-farming, and the construction of other medieval churches seems to have been supported by rents from arable farming. The power of the medieval church, and the risk of invasion, however, both ended within fifty years, with the Reformation of 1560 followed by the Union of the Crowns in 1603.

Turning at last to looking at the religious buildings themselves, the Border abbeys are unquestionably the great glories, in architectural terms, of the whole area. Founded in the earlier stages of the feudal reforms of landownership in Scotland, the abbeys were part of David I's strategy for the Church, which appears

Fig. 5. Prestonpans Parish Church,
East Lothian

Fig. 6. Cockburnspath Parish Church, Scottish Borders

to have been to use it as a moderating influence on the great landowners and their families. The most complete of the Border abbey churches is Jedburgh. It shares with Kelso a fundamentally Romanesque character. Kelso, in its heyday the largest abbey church in Scotland, is now reduced to a fragment of the west end – but a monumental one, impressing by the vigour of its massing and detailing. Dryburgh is also much reduced; its beauty as a ruin is much enhanced by its unspoilt rural setting. Melrose is also fragmentary and may never have been completed in its ultimately designed form. The church has some of the finest and most appealing details of any medieval building in Scotland, and is complemented by significant remains of the other buildings of the monastery. Sir Walter Scott wrote of it: 'If thou would see fair Melrose aright, go visit it by the pale moonlight' – but the subtlety of its design and craftsmanship are best seen in daylight. There is humour there too – for instance the sculpture, on the nave, of a pig with bagpipes.

As with other large medieval churches in Scotland, all of these buildings except Dryburgh were adapted for Reformed worship after the Reformation. In Jedburgh, parts of the abbey church were used as the parish church until 1875. The west end of Kelso was similarly used until a new parish church opened in 1773, ensuring its survival into modern times. The most drastic alteration was at Melrose, where a new barrel vault was inserted into the east end of the nave, which was walled off from the rest of the church. A very obviously Reformed belfry was also placed on top of the gable of the south transept. The abbeys, now in the care of Historic Scotland, were among the first tourist attractions in Scotland, and Melrose alone generated much of the passenger traffic on the Hawick Branch of the North British Railway after 1850. To this day, their remains are intensely evocative of the

Fig. 7. Former burial aisle, Oldhamstocks Parish Church, East Lothian

Fig. 8. The ruined former North Berwick Parish Church, East Lothian

place of the medieval church in the totality of Scottish culture, and of a distinctive approach to spirituality.

Medieval churches of more modest character are also well represented throughout the Borders and East Lothian. Scarcely more modest than the abbey churches is St Mary's, Haddington (**15**), a large cruciform burgh church of the fourteenth century, sacked in 1548. The nave of this building was restored and used as the parish church after the Reformation, and the choir remained roofless until 1973, when it was restored with fibreglass 'vaulting'. The Cross Kirk, Peebles, now a roofless ruin, dates in part from about 1260 and was extended in the mid-fifteenth century. Whitekirk (**38**), a smaller fifteenth-century cruciform building, was burned by suffragettes in 1914 but subsequently restored. The later pre-Reformation churches at Dunglass (mid-fifteenth century, Fig. 1) and Seton (fifteenth–sixteenth century, Fig. 2) were built to be served by groups of priests – colleges – who were paid to say prayers for the souls of the patron and his family. Both buildings are in the care of Historic Scotland. Seton has a polygonal apse, a distinctive feature of late Scots Gothic church-building; and St Mary's, Ladykirk (**57**, c. 1500; still in use for worship) has a chancel apse and also canted ends to the transepts. Like Seton, it has a stone-slab roof, another distinctive feature of building of that period.

The shells of these churches have all remained largely unaltered since they were first completed. Most of the other pre-Reformation churches in the area have, however, evolved since their initial construction, so that defining what is genuinely ancient can be challenging. Stobo Kirk (**80**), Linton (**112**) and Legerwood (**59**) all have significant amounts of twelfth-century work, and a twelfth-century doorway has been incorporated into the more altered building at Chirnside (**44**). There is also twelfth-century fabric in Garvald. At Edrom (**51**) and Bonkyl (**63**),

Fig. 9. The ruined former Gladsmuir Parish Church, East Lothian

Fig. 10. The former Polwarth Parish Church, Scottish Borders

semi-circular twelfth-century apses have been preserved in churchyards associated with later buildings. Much of Coldingham Priory Church (**45**) dates from the thirteenth century, but it was rebuilt in the 1660s and again in the 1850s. Parts of Abbey St Bathan's (**40**, also originally a priory) also date from the thirteenth century, and there is a thirteenth-century window in Cockburnspath (Fig. 6), which is otherwise much later. Other churches with notable medieval fabric include Prestonkirk, East Linton (**32**, now part of the parish of Traprain), which has a very fine thirteenth-century Gothic chancel; Aberlady, with a fifteenth-century tower; and Pencaitland (**30**), a really difficult building to decipher. There is also medieval fabric in Drumelzier (**69**) and more recognisably at Bowden (**87**, fifteenth century). The tower of St Andrew's Old Church, Peebles (also briefly a collegiate church), probably of the sixteenth century, survives but was extensively restored in 1883. The ruined nave of St Martin's, Haddington (twelfth century, Fig. 3), though original in form, has been stripped of its dressed stone, and it is impossible to recreate its original appearance. Some of the other roofless ruins in the area are also, at least in part, pre-Reformation. These include the remains of a little chapel at North Berwick harbour (Fig. 4) and the old church of Gullane. The most striking and arguably most important ruin of a smaller church is, however, Tyninghame (in the grounds of Tyninghame House). Here, only the skeleton and lower walls survive of a three-compartment twelfth-century Romanesque parish church, which survived in use until 1761. When complete, this would have been similar to Dalmeny and Leuchars parish churches.

Few churches seem to have been built in Scotland in the years immediately following the Reformation. One of the most complete of these is in our area: Prestonpans, a considerable part of which dates from 1595 (Fig. 5). As with so many of the earlier churches in East Lothian

Fig. 11. Morham Parish Church, East Lothian

Fig. 12. Duns Parish Church, Scottish Borders

and the Borders, however, it has been much remodelled since its initial construction. The medieval church of Cockburnspath appears to have been rebuilt in the late sixteenth century, when it gained the lower stages of its distinctive round tower (Fig. 6). The Reformed Church of Scotland banned burials in church buildings, and thus private burial aisles were constructed by landowning families as extensions of existing church buildings. A good early example in our area is at Oldhamstocks (1581; now a chancel, Fig. 7). During the seventeenth century, several fine churches were built in the area, and three are relatively little altered. These are Dirleton (**6**, 1612), Lauder (**58**, 1673) and Greenlaw (**56**, c. 1675). At first sight, Dirleton and Greenlaw seem similar – long rectangular buildings with western towers. Greenlaw's tower was, however, originally detached from the church and was the place's tolbooth. Dirleton has a superb burial aisle, the Archerfield Aisle (1664), on its south wall. Other seventeenth-century aisles, at Spott and Fogo, are much plainer. The third of this group, Lauder, is a late and perfect example of the equal-armed Greek-cross plan favoured by the Church of Scotland in the seventeenth century. It was built as the estate church for the Duke of Lauderdale's Thirlestane estate. Lyne Church (**74**, c. 1645) is much smaller than these, and probably representative of smaller seventeenth-century country churches. It was, however, significantly altered in two stages during the nineteenth century. So, too, was Mertoun (**62**, 1652), whose proportions and belfry are seventeenth-century, but which was Gothicised, probably in 1820. Parts of Bowden also date from the seventeenth century, including the Roxburghe (1644) and Cavers (1661) aisles. Cavers Old Church (1662) survives, though no longer a church. Other seventeenth-century remains can be found at Prestonkirk and Pencaitland (where the very different towers both date from 1631), and at North Berwick Old (1664; now roofless and decaying,

Fig. 13. Eccles Parish Church, Scottish Borders

Fig. 14. Tranent Old,
East Lothian

Fig. 8), where there is a tower, added in 1770, similar to that of Prestonkirk. Seventeenth-century fabric also survives in Smailholm (**125**, originally medieval, rebuilt 1632) and Yarrow (**130**, 1640), both subsequently much rebuilt. The roofless remains of the old church of Gladsmuir (1697, Fig. 9) give a clear idea of the character of the churches built for the Church of Scotland in the years immediately following the restoration of Presbyterianism in 1690 after James II was deposed from the throne of the United Kingdom.

As elsewhere in Scotland, there was much quickening of economic activity in East Lothian and the Borders during the eighteenth century, and hence much rebuilding and new building of churches, both in towns and villages and in the countryside. There are two early eighteenth-century churches of national importance in the area, Polwarth (1703, Fig. 10) and Yester (**12**, 1710). Both have tall towers and slated spires and are harled. Oldhamstocks (1701) is a more modest but delightful building, typical in scale of many of the country churches of the eighteenth century. Later examples are Skirling (**79**, 1720), Morham (1724, Fig. 11), Oxnam (**122**, 1738), Roxburgh (**123**, 1752), Stichill (**129**, 1780s), Innerwick (1784), Spott (**34**, 1790) and Ashkirk (1791). Most of these have round-headed windows, rare elsewhere in Scotland until the later eighteenth century. As the majority of these buildings, however, have been altered during their long lives, the extent to which these windows are original remains for this author a debatable question. Some of the eighteenth-century country churches have been more radically altered than these. Whittingehame (**39**, 1722) has been dressed up as an early nineteenth-century 'Heritors' Gothic' building; and Longformacus (**61**, 1730), Lilliesleaf (**111**, 1771) and Athelstaneford (**2**, 1780) at first glance look like Victorian buildings. Fogo (**52**) is notable for its largely unaltered

Fig. 15. Cavers Parish Church,
Scottish Borders

Fig. 16. Gladsmuir Parish Church, East Lothian

interior, with a canopied pulpit, and for its generally Georgian appearance. It is, however, as *The Buildings of Scotland: Borders* points out, an assemblage of fabric from the twelfth century (lower walls), 1683 (burial aisle, upper walls and jamb), 1755 (some windows and belfry) and 1853 (alterations including some windows). Nothing is simple in deciphering the history of the rural churches of East Lothian and the Borders.

Other notable eighteenth-century churches are to be found in the towns. The shell of St Mary's and Old, Hawick (**96**) dates largely from 1764 and has a resemblance to Yester. Kelso Old (**104**, 1773, built to house the congregation removed from the abbey church) is the area's only polygonal church, a layout in vogue at that time. Duns Old (1790, Fig. 12) and Coldstream (1795) were both built with fashionable classical steeples, but in both cases the bodies of the churches were subsequently rebuilt. Two other eighteenth-century urban churches are primarily of historical interest. The first part of Dunbar Methodist Church (**10**) dates from 1764, and Holy Trinity Scottish Episcopal Church, Haddington (**16**) from 1770. Both are early churches for their denomination. Eccles (1774, Fig. 13), though not in a town, is urban in scale and sophistication.

The mixture of vernacular and classical that had characterised church-building in East Lothian and the Borders in the seventeenth and eighteenth centuries broke down in the early nineteenth century. Three fine classical churches were built between 1800 and 1812, but the Gothic was beginning to become fashionable. These classical churches are St Michael's, Inveresk (**18**, 1805), the largest and finest, serving a select suburb of Edinburgh as well as a thriving burgh, with a superb, assured classical steeple. The parish church of Melrose (**115**), built in 1808–10 to accommodate the congregation which had been meeting in the abbey church, also has a classical steeple, the only part of that building to survive a fire in 1908. The former Eyemouth Old (1812; now Eyemouth Museum) is a

Fig. 17. Hutton Parish Church, Scottish Borders

Fig. 18. Cockenzie Parish Church,
East Lothian

freer composition, with a cupola instead of a steeple. Whitsome (**67**, 1803) and Makerstoun (**113**, 1808) are only Gothic in having pointed arches, but Tranent Old (1800, Fig. 14) and Bolton (**4**, 1809) have pinnacled end towers in the manner of the slightly later fully fledged 'Heritors' Gothic'. Saltoun (**11**, 1805) is unique in Scotland, with a slender steeple rising from a squat tower – a very engaging building, set in woodland which throws into relief the spikiness of the church's profile.

In the later 1810s and 1820s, Heritors' Gothic became fashionable. Channelkirk (**43**, 1817) is a fine example, but unusual in having a belfry instead of a tower; it has a particularly fine, unaltered interior. The adaptation of Whittingehame (**39**) to conform to the new fashion took place in 1820, and the first all-new church in this style in the area was Dunbar (**7**, 1821), a particularly fine and elaborate example. Cavers (1822, Fig. 15) is in a local, rather clumsy, variant on the style; and Ettrick and Buccleuch (**91**, 1824) uses the form, but not the Gothic detail, of the type. This church has a good, little-altered interior. Stenton (**35**, 1829) appears at first sight to be a typical Heritors' Gothic church but is, unusually, on a T-plan. It is also a very refined design. The last church in a variant on this style is the idiosyncratic Kirk Yetholm (**109**, 1836–7), notable for the dark whinstone of which it is constructed. At Minto (**118**, 1830), the pinnacled tower is replaced by a crenellated one, giving a more settled appearance.

Other styles were introduced in the 1830s. Eddleston (**70**) is in a form of Tudor Gothic; and Northesk, Musselburgh (**19**, 1835) uses round-headed arches in a distinctive manner. Gladsmuir (1838, Fig. 16) is in the same style as Northesk. Hutton (1835, Fig. 17) is the earliest true Romanesque Revival church, not just in the area but in the whole of Scotland. The classical steeple made its last

Fig. 19. The former Wishart Church of
Scotland, Tranent, East Lothian

appearance at Belhaven, Dunbar (**3**, 1838–40), but in juxtaposition to Gothic windows. St Peter's Scottish Episcopal Church, Peebles (**77**, 1836) is in a simple and pleasing version of the 'English College Chapel' style, where the architectural interest is concentrated on the street-frontage gable. Houndwood (1836; now disused) was built, uniquely, in an Italianate style; and Cockenzie (1838, Fig. 18) is in a simple Tudor style.

Fig. 20. The former Dunbar Free Church, East Lothian

The eighteenth-century secessions which strongly influenced many parts of Scotland seem to have had relatively little impact on East Lothian and the Borders. There is a former Glasite church in Galashiels (1842), in Haddington a Secession church of 1808 (off Market Street); and in Jedburgh there are the former Relief (1818; now British Legion Hall) and Blackfriars (Secession, 1818) churches. A Secession church that is still in use for worship is Leitholm Parish Church (**60**, 1835, Original Secession); and in Tranent the former Wishart Church was built in about 1830 as a United Secession church (Fig. 19). It is a rarity in the area in being classical in design. In 1820, many of the Secession churches came together as the United Secession Church, and in 1847 this amalgamated with the Relief Church to form the United Presbyterian Church – one of the major denominations in later nineteenth-century Scotland, and particularly powerful in town and cities. A more far-reaching event was the Disruption in 1843, when the Church of Scotland split over the right of congregations to choose their own ministers. About a third of ministers walked out of the General Assembly and immediately formed the Free Church. This was less influential in the Borders and East Lothian than in other parts of Scotland, but still a significant force. These three churches, Church of Scotland, Free and United Presbyterian, dominated church-building in

Fig. 21. The former St Andrew's Church of Scotland, East Linton, East Lothian

Fig. 22. Haddington West Parish Church, East Lothian

the area in the second half of the nineteenth century, but numbers of churches were also built by the Scottish Episcopal and Roman Catholic churches.

The new Free Church was immediately faced with finding accommodation for congregations who had left the Church of Scotland. It is remarkable how quickly new buildings were put up. In our area, the present St Boswells Parish Church was originally a Free church (**128**, 1844), as was Denholm Church (**89**, 1845). The former Dunbar Free Church (1850; now a hall, Fig. 20) is more elaborate, with a spirelet. As the new denomination gained strength, many of the pioneer churches were replaced by larger and more elaborate buildings. All the major denominations favoured the Gothic Revival, and it is notable that no classical churches were built in the area after 1812.

The Scottish Episcopal Church began building numbers of new churches in East Lothian and the Borders in the 1840s and 1850s. St John the Evangelist, Jedburgh (**102**, 1844) was the first, followed by Holy Trinity, Melrose (**116**, 1846–50), St Mungo's, West Linton (**84**, 1851), St Peter's, Galashiels (**94**, 1853), Christ Church, Duns (**49**, 1853–4) and St Cuthbert's, Hawick (**97**, 1858). Most of these are relatively small, simple Gothic churches, but the Duns church is larger, with a massive tower. St John the Evangelist has a richly decorated interior, with furnishings influenced by the Tractarian movement in the Church of England. This movement sought to re-establish pre-Reformation styles of worship. The construction of these buildings reflected the general revival of Episcopalianism, with its closer

Fig. 23. The former Musselburgh High Church of Scotland, East Lothian

Fig. 24. Trinity Church, Galashiels,
Scottish Borders

alignment with Anglicanism and a movement of members of the Church of England into the area. Construction of Episcopal churches continued into the 1860s, with St Baldred's, North Berwick (**24**, 1861, 1863), St Peter's, Musselburgh (**21**, 1865), St Andrew's, Kelso (**106**, 1867–9) and St John's, Selkirk (1867–9). St Baldred's is unusual in being Romanesque, with apsidal ends to the chancel and south aisle, while St Peter's and St Andrew's both have steeples. St Andrew's is an early work of Sir Robert Rowand Anderson, and a particularly effective design. It replaced an Episcopal church of 1764, a very early foundation. Roman Catholicism was not strong in the area, but small new churches were built for that denomination in Peebles (St Joseph, **78**, 1858) and Kelso (The Immaculate Conception, **103**, 1858).

The steeples on St Peter's, Musselburgh and St Andrew's, Kelso can be seen as a part of a growing fashion in Gothic Revival architecture to incorporate such features, and also a sign of the growing wealth of the area. The fashion came late to East Lothian and the Borders. An early and conventional Church of Scotland example is Ayton Parish Church (**41**, 1864–6). Its near-contemporary, Kelso North (**105**, Free, 1865–7), is much more innovative, an example of the original approach of F. T. Pilkington to the Gothic. Innerleithen Parish Church (**71**, 1864–7), also by Pilkington, was designed to be equally striking, but was not completed as intended and was subsequently modified.

Subsequent steepled Gothic Revival churches were mostly more conventional, and included, for the Free Church, Peebles (1871–2; now an arts centre) and the former Ladhope Free, Galashiels (1884–5; now an arts centre, with its steeple cut down); and, for the United Presbyterian Church, Peebles

Fig. 25. The former Gullane United Free Church,
East Lothian

Fig. 26. The former Coldstream United Free Church, Scottish Borders

Leckie Memorial (**76**, 1875–7) and the present Selkirk Parish Church (1878–80). The Roman Catholics built St James's, Innerleithen (**73**) in 1881. Gothic steeples were features of several Church of Scotland churches of the period, notably Langton Parish, Gavinton (**54**, 1872), Jedburgh Parish (1872–5, replacing the abbey church), Tweedsmuir (**83**, 1874–5) and – the largest and finest – Galashiels Old and St Paul's (**93**, 1878–81, steeple 1886). Tweedsmuir's spire overhangs its supporting tower, giving an odd, top-heavy appearance. The former St Andrew's, East Linton (ex-Free, 1879, Fig. 21) has a unique slated spire.

By the 1880s, the fashion for conventional Gothic steeples was waning, and towers were becoming popular for larger churches. St Andrew Blackadder, North Berwick (**26**, 1882), Kelso United Presbyterian Church (1885–6; no longer a church) and Haddington West (ex-Free, 1890, Fig. 22) all have powerful towers. So, too, has the former Musselburgh High (ex-Free, enlarged 1889; now a museum, Fig. 23), in a very different style. The tower of Peebles Old (**75**, 1885–7) has a crown steeple in keeping with its generally late Scots Gothic style. Not all of the larger Gothic churches had steeples or towers. Abbey (**25**, 1868, United Presbyterian) and Walkerburn (1875, 1891, Church of Scotland; no longer in use) are examples of sizeable churches of this character. A unique church is Trinity Church, Galashiels (1879–80, Fig. 24), on a confined town-centre site with a carefully detailed Byzantine gable.

While in the towns and larger villages big Gothic Revival churches were being constructed, the building of smaller churches continued. Most of these were generally Gothic in style. Hobkirk (**99**, 1862), with its squat tower capped by parapets with open bartizans at the corners, is particularly pleasing. Others include Newtown St Boswells (**121**, 1866–7, United Presbyterian) and, for the Church of Scotland, Saughtree (**124**, 1872), Manor (**110**, 1874), Southdean (**126**, 1876), Edrom (**51**, 1884–5), Newcastleton (**120**, 1888) and Ancrum (**85**, 1890). The Roman Catholics built small churches in Dunbar (**9**, Our Lady of the Waves, 1877) and North Berwick (**27**, Our Lady, Star of the Sea, 1879), and the Scottish Episcopal Church constructed St Anne's, Dunbar (**8**) in 1890.

Fig. 27. St Ninian's Parish Church, Musselburgh, East Lothian

Alongside the construction of new churches, older ones were being rebuilt and extended. These included Drumelzier (**69**, 1872), Chirnside (**44**, 1878) and Morebattle (**119**, 1899). After the turn of the century, both of the latter were further altered, in 1904–7 and 1903 respectively; and Lilliesleaf (**111**) was radically transformed in 1910. Yarrow (**130**), a complex building dating in part from the seventeenth century, was substantially remodelled in 1906.

Towards the end of the nineteenth century, the architectural styles of the high Victorian period came under scrutiny. An early example of this in East Lothian and the Borders was the little church at Gullane (**13**, 1887) in a refreshingly simple Norman style. A more elaborate Romanesque Revival church is Cranshaws (**48**, 1899), with a notable interior incorporating a semi-circular chancel and a laird's pew with separate external access. Bonkyl (**63**, 1905), by the same designer, is also Romanesque, but here the style is more freely interpreted. All three of these churches were built for the Church of Scotland. So, too, was the little Hoselaw Chapel (**100**), a tiny but beautiful Romanesque building by the doyen of Romanesque Revival architects, Peter Macgregor Chalmers, who also restored the partly twelfth-century Linton Parish Church (**112**). Wilton Parish Church, Hawick (a building of 1860–2) was much enlarged in 1908–10 to create a complex impressive in its clarity of design. The union of the Free and the United Presbyterian Churches in 1900 did not have the same impact on the area as in other parts of Scotland, but resulted in the construction of two important churches in East Lothian. Marginally the more orthodox of these is the former Gullane United Free Church (1908 and earlier; now a house, Fig. 25), with its dominant tower and complex short slated spire. The more remarkable is the Chalmers Memorial Church at Port Seton (**31**, 1904), with an eye-catching exterior but with a breathtaking and highly original interior. The roof timbers are painted with stencilled decoration; and the

Fig. 28. St Gabriel's Roman Catholic Church, Prestonpans, East Lothian

fittings and stained glass, though modest, are of the highest quality. In the author's view, this is one of the finest churches of any period in Scotland. Coldstream United Free Church (1907; now a church centre, Fig. 26) is more conventional, with a handsome tower. St Andrew's Scottish Episcopal Church, Innerleithen (**72**, 1904) is an immensely pleasing simple building. In 1905, Our Lady of Loretto, Musselburgh (**22**) was built for the Roman Catholic Church. The last churches in the area to be completed before the First World War brought a stop to church-building were St Mary and All Souls Scottish Episcopal Church, Coldstream (**47**, 1913–14) and Bedrule Parish Church (**86**, 1914). The latter was a substantial rebuilding of older fabric, and is similar in massing to Hobkirk but with late Scots Gothic detailing. The Coldstream church is notable for its semi-circular apse.

After the First World War, there was little need for new churches in the area. Longniddry Parish Church was built in about 1920 as part of a postwar housing development, and a fire in Yarrow Kirk (**130**) in 1922 necessitated its rebuilding. St Adrian's Scottish Episcopal Church, Gullane (**14**) was constructed in 1926, and the Roman Catholic Church built a delightfully plain church in Jedburgh (St Mary's, **103**, 1937). The last new Church of Scotland church in the area to be built before the outbreak of the Second World War was Ormiston (**29**, 1938). Like other interwar churches in the area, its design was deceptively simple.

Even after the Second World War, few churches were required. Nunraw Abbey (**28**), a Cistercian monastery, was founded in 1952 and built between then and 1970. The original design contemplated the construction of a free-standing church, but in the event a chapel was formed within the conventual buildings. Church Extension within the Church of Scotland resulted in the construction of three churches in new housing areas. The first of these was Burnfoot Parish Church (1953–5) in a new suburb of Hawick. St Ninian's, Musselburgh (1955, Fig. 27) is at Levenhall on the eastern outskirts of the town, and St John's, Galashiels (1970–1) is in Easter Langlee, to the south-east of the town centre, developed as a housing estate from 1967. The most distinctive postwar churches are Roman Catholic. The church of St Martin of Tours, Tranent (**36**, 1969), replacing an earlier building, is on an octagonal plan, typical of many postwar Roman Catholic churches. The finest postwar church in the area is arguably St Gabriel's, Prestonpans (1965, Fig. 28), on a circular plan.

There is an extraordinary variety of church buildings in East Lothian and the Borders, as rich as any in Scotland. Relics of the earliest period of stone church-construction in Scotland are numerous. So, too, is evidence of the richness and virtuosity of later medieval designers and craftsmen, particularly in the ruins of the Border abbeys. The parish churches are also well worth visiting, often revealing alteration over many centuries. Many of the older buildings also evoke the uncertainties of relations between Scotland and England before the Union of the Crowns in 1603. Then there are the churches of the seventeenth and eighteenth centuries, of the transition to a modern society, and those of the Victorian heyday of the Scottish economy and of denominational rivalry.

Finally, there are the twentieth-century buildings, few in number but reminding us of important social developments and of those that bypassed the area. All of these speak of belief rooted in the land – for it is the land that has generated most of these churches, a land rich in associations of all kinds. Visitors have for generations made pilgrimages round the Border abbeys, but one can also seek out buildings that trace many different pieces of the story of belief. Even the abbeys have their tales to tell of Reformation as well as of a vanished medieval past. There are many notions of sacredness embodied in the churches of the Borders and East Lothian. Bring imagination and perception, go and investigate; in no way will you be disappointed. Riches, spiritual and material, await you.

PROFESSOR JOHN R. HUME
Universities of Glasgow and St Andrews

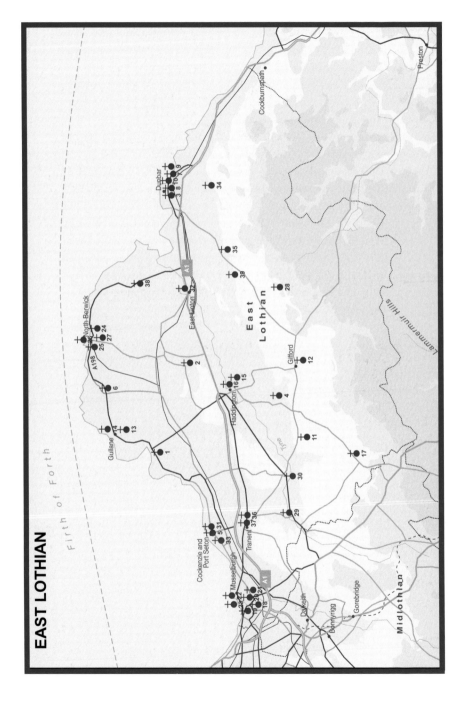

EAST LOTHIAN

Firth of Forth

Preston

Cockburnspath

East Lothian

Lammermuir Hills

Dunbar

34

35

39

28

38

A1

East Linton 32

North Berwick

A198

24
27
25

Gifford

12

2

A1

6

Haddington 16
15

4

Gullane
14
13

Tyne

11

1

17

30

29

Cockenzie and
Port Seton

5 31
33

37 36

Tranent

Musselburgh

A1

Dalkeith

Midlothian

Gorebridge

Bonnyrigg

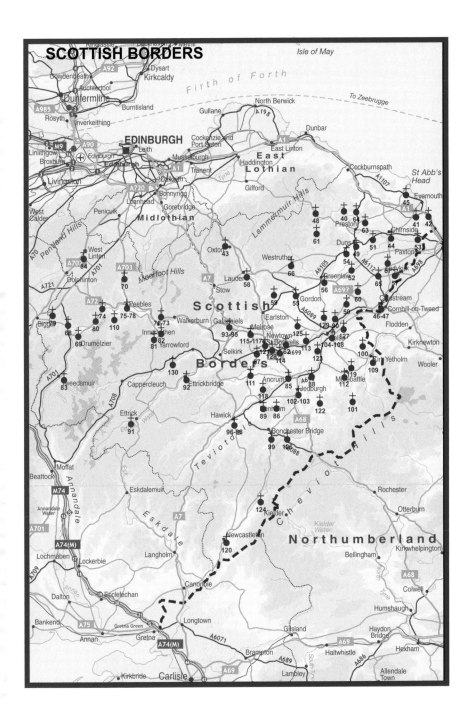

How to use this Guide

Entries are arranged by local-authority area, with large areas sub-divided for convenience. The number preceding each entry refers to the map. Each entry is followed by symbols for access and facilities:

Ⅰ	Ordnance Survey reference	ᨐ	Hearing induction loop for the deaf
🏠	Denomination	👤	Welcomers and guides on duty
🌐	Church website	📖	Guidebooks and souvenirs available/for sale
●	Regular services		
○	Church events	NADFAS	Church Recorders' Inventory (NADFAS)
●	Opening arrangements	ⓨ	Features for children/link with schools
♿	Wheelchair access for partially abled	■	Refreshments
WC	Toilets available for visitors	Ⓐ	Category A listing
WC	Toilets adapted for the disabled available for visitors	Ⓑ	Category B listing
		Ⓒ	Category C listing

Category A: Buildings of national or international importance, either architectural or historic, or fine little-altered examples of some particular period, style or building type.

Category B: Buildings of regional or more than local importance, or major examples of some particular period, style or building type which may have been altered.

Category C: Buildings of local importance, lesser examples of any period, style, or building type, as originally constructed or moderately altered; and simple traditional buildings which group well with others in categories A and B.

The information appearing in the gazetteer of this guide is supplied by the participating churches. While this is believed to be correct at the time of going to press, Scotland's Churches Scheme cannot accept any responsibility for its accuracy.

EAST LOTHIAN

❶ ABERLADY PARISH CHURCH

Main Street
Aberlady
EH32 0RE

⚔ NT 462 799

⛪ Church of Scotland

Linked with Gullane Parish Church (13)

All that remains of the 15th-century church is the tower; the body of the church was rebuilt in 1773 and recast in 1886 by William Young, who added two aisles on the south to match the post-Reformation burial aisles on the north. Stained glass by Edward Frampton, London 1889. Eighth-century cross. Marble monument attributed to Canova.

- Sunday: 11.15am
- Open May to September, 8.00am to dusk or by arrangement (01875 853137)

❷ ATHELSTANEFORD PARISH CHURCH

Athelstaneford
EH39 5BE

⚔ NT 533 774

⛪ Church of Scotland

Linked with St Mary's Parish Church, Whitekirk (38)

On B1343, 3km (2 miles) north of A1

The original church, 'Ecclesia de Elstaneford', on this site is said to have been founded in 1176 by the Countess Ada, mother of William the Lion. The present church dates from 1780. Cruciform design with central aisle, transepts and semi-octagonal chancel. Bellcote on the west gable. Three stained-glass windows by C. E. Kempe. Doocot 1583. Church has historic link with the Scottish saltire: commemorative plaque and saltire floodlit. Heritage Centre to rear of church opened in 1997 with audiovisual display (entry free).

- Sunday: 10.00am
- Open daily, 9.00am–6.00pm (01620 880339)

❸ BELHAVEN PARISH CHURCH

**Edinburgh Road
Dunbar
EH42 1NH**

⚲ NT 668 788

⛪ Church of Scotland

🌐 www.belhavenparishchurch.org.uk

Linked with Spott Parish Church (34)

Built 1838–40 in red whinstone with sandstone dressings and tower, the church occupies a prominent position, with halls to the rear in extensive community use. Chancel windows depict Angels of Peace, Faith, Hope and Sacrifice. Pipe organ by Forster & Andrews. Seasonal banners are displayed. A warm welcome to all visitors.

- Sunday: 11.30am
- Open by arrangement (01368 863098)

❹ BOLTON PARISH CHURCH

**Bolton
EH41 4HL**

⚲ NT 507 701

⛪ Church of Scotland

🌐 http://ndhm.org.uk

Linked with Saltoun Parish Church (11), Yester Parish Church, Gifford (12), Humbie Kirk (17)

B6368 from Haddington

There has been a church on this site since before 1244. The present building dates from 1809 and has remained structurally unchanged since that time. The architect was probably Archibald Elliot. The interior is plain and unspoiled, complete with carpenter's Gothic pulpit, and gallery on clustered iron posts. Robert Burns's mother, brother and sisters are buried in the churchyard. Graveguard and other items dating from the time of the 'Resurrection Men' displayed in the porch.

- Sunday: 10.00am, alternating with Saltoun
- Open daily (01620 810515)

⑤ COCKENZIE METHODIST CHURCH

**28 Edinburgh Road
Cockenzie
EH32 0JA**

Å NT 398 756

⛪ Methodist

Linked with Dunbar Methodist Church (10), Tranent Methodist Church (37)

South side of main road at west end of village

The third of East Lothian's three Primitive Methodist Chapels, 1878. Simple and attractive stone building with round-headed windows and a porch. Fully modernised, 2007, with comfortable chairs and warm ambience. A warm welcome for local folk and visitors alike.

- Sunday: 2.30pm
- Open by arrangement (01875 811137 or 01875 813017)

⑥ DIRLETON KIRK

**Manse Road
Dirleton
EH39 5EH**

Å NT 513 842

⛪ Church of Scotland

🌐 www.abbeychurch.co.uk

Linked with Abbey Church, North Berwick (25)

North side of village

Attractive stone building erected in 1612 to replace 12th-century kirk in Gullane which was 'continewallie overblawin with sand'. Archerfield Aisle added 1650 – first example of neoclassical design in Scotland. Tower crowned with Gothic pinnacles in 1836. Interesting examples of stained glass, including *St Francis and the Animals*, Margaret Chilton 1936. The church looks onto the attractive village green.

- Sunday: 9.30am
- Open daily, 10.00am to dusk (01620 892800)

7 DUNBAR PARISH CHURCH

Queen's Road
Dunbar
EH42 1LB

⚐ NT 682 786

🏛 Church of Scotland

🌐 www.dunbarparishchurch.org

200 metres south of the High Street

The building, designed by Gillespie Graham in 1821, has been beautifully reconstructed by Campbell & Arnott in 1990 following a devastating fire in 1987. The colourful and modern interior includes the early 17th-century monument to the Earl of Dunbar and some fine stained glass by Shona McInnes and Douglas Hogg, 1990.

- Sunday: 11.00am
- Open during daylight hours (01368 863316)

8 ST ANNE'S CHURCH, DUNBAR

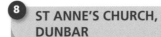

Westgate
Dunbar
EH42 1JL

⚐ NT 678 791

🏛 Scottish Episcopal

🌐 www.stannesdunbar.org.uk

North end of High Street

Designed by Hew Maitland Wardrop and executed by Robert Rowand Anderson, 1890. Gothic Revival-style church with fine Scots detail. Carved oak furnishings by Robert Lorimer. Henry Willis organ. Stained glass by Ballantine & Gardiner, Heaton, Butler & Bayne, and the Abbey Studio.

- Sunday: 9.15am (except 1st Sunday of the month) and 10.30am; Thursday: 10.30am
- Open by arrangement (01368 865711 or 01368 863335)

⑨ OUR LADY OF THE WAVES, DUNBAR

**Westgate
Dunbar
EH42 1JL**

 NT 678 791

Roman Catholic

🌐 www.nbstar.org.uk

Built in 1877 of grey freestone in the 'Early Decorated' Gothic style by Dunn & Hansom. The church comprises a well-furnished nave leading through the chancel arch to a taller sanctuary. Stained glass behind the altar; wood carvings show the Way of the Cross. Silver sanctuary lamp in the shape of a ship.

- Saturday: Vigil 6.30pm; Sunday: 10.30am; Mass: Monday, Tuesday, Wednesday and Friday 9.30am and Thursday 7.00am
- Open daily (01620 892195)

⑩ DUNBAR METHODIST CHURCH

**10 Victoria Street
Dunbar
EH42 1ET**

 NT 679 791

Methodist

🌐 www.dunbar.uko2.co.uk/

Linked with Cockenzie Methodist Church (5), Tranent Methodist Church (37)

South side of road leading from High Street to harbour

Scotland's oldest Methodist Church, built 1764. John and Charles Wesley were trustees, and John often preached here. Enlarged 1857, renovated 1890. Fine interior, unexpected from plain exterior. Oak pulpit. Stained-glass windows from St Giles' Cathedral, Edinburgh.

- Sunday: 11.00am and 7.00pm
- Open by arrangement (01368 862052)

11 SALTOUN PARISH CHURCH, EAST SALTOUN

**East Saltoun
EH34 5EE**

NT 474 678

Church of Scotland

http://ndhm.org.uk

Linked with Bolton Parish Church (4), Yester Parish Church, Gifford (12), Humbie Kirk (17)

B6355, 5km (3 miles) south-east of Pencaitland

There has been a church on this site since before 1244. The present building is a T-plan Gothic kirk of 1805 which John Fletcher Campbell built 'as a monument to the virtues of his ancestors'. The actual designer is most likely to have been Robert Burn. The interior was recast in 1885; the architect was John Lessels. Beneath the church lies the Fletcher Vault, containing the remains of Andrew Fletcher, 'The Patriot', and members of his family.

- Sunday: 10.00am, alternating with Bolton
- Open by arrangement (01620 810515)

 12 YESTER PARISH CHURCH, GIFFORD

**Main Street
Gifford
EH41 4QH**

NT 535 681

Church of Scotland

Linked with Bolton Parish Church (4), Saltoun Parish Church (11), Humbie Kirk (17)

B6369 from Haddington

By James Smith, finished 1710. A white-harled T-plan church with square staged tower and slated-spire. Weathervane in the form of a heron by William Brown, Edinburgh 1709. Church bell from the old Church of Bothans 1492. Pulpit 17th-century with bracket for baptismal basin. Memorial in village wall opposite to Rev. John Witherspoon, son of the manse, who signed the American Declaration of Independence 1784.

- Sunday: 11.30am
- Open 9.00am–5.00pm April to October (01620 810515)

EAST LOTHIAN

13 GULLANE PARISH CHURCH

St Andrew's

**East Links Road
Gullane
EH31 2AF**

⚔ NT 480 827

🏛 Church of Scotland

Linked with Aberlady Parish
Church (1)

A198

The church, designed by Glasgow
architect John Honeyman and
completed in 1888, replaced an earlier
12th-century building vacated in
1612 when the congregation was
rehoused in a new kirk at Dirleton.
The Kirk Session of Dirleton decided
to build the present parish church
for the benefit of 'the large number
of summer visitors annually residing
in the village'. Simple Norman
style with east apse. The zig-zagged
chancel arch is derived from the
old parish church, as is the south
doorway, whose tympanum has a low
relief of St Andrew. Murray Memorial
windows with beautiful painted glass
by John Clark, 2003.

- Sunday: 9.45am
- Open daily, 9.00am–5.00pm (01620
  843192)

14 ST ADRIAN'S CHURCH, GULLANE

**Sandy Loan
Gullane
EH31 2BH**

⚔ NT 480 838

🏛 Scottish Episcopal

🌐 www.edinburgh.anglican.org

Linked with St Baldred's Church,
North Berwick (24)

Beach road at west end of village

A simple aisleless church in Arts and
Crafts style by Reginald Fairlie, 1926.
Built of stone from the Rattlebag
quarry, with a low tower and slated
pyramidal spire. Three-light chancel
window by Douglas Strachan, 1934.

- Sunday: 9.30am, 8.00am on 1st and
  3rd Sunday of the month
- Open April to September 10.00am–
  5.00pm or by arrangement (01620
  892154)

15 ST MARY'S PARISH CHURCH, HADDINGTON

The Lamp of Lothian

**Sidegate
Haddington
EH41 4BZ**

NT 519 736

Church of Scotland

www.stmaryskirk.com

Dating back to the 14th century, one of the three great pre-Reformation churches of the Lothians. Used as the parish church for almost 400 years. Nave repaired for John Knox and the Reformers after Siege of Haddington 1548. Transepts and choir restored, Ian G. Lindsay & Partners, 1973. Lauderdale Aisle, now the Chapel of the Three Kings, in regular ecumenical use. Fine stone carvings, notable stained glass by Sir Edward Burne-Jones and Sax Shaw. Modern tapestries. Pipe organ by Lammermuir Pipe Organs, 1990. A peal of eight bells installed in 1999.

- Sunday: 9.30am and 11.00am
- Open May to September, Monday to Saturday, 11.00am–4.00pm, Sunday 2.00–4.30pm or by arrangement (01620 825111)

16 HOLY TRINITY CHURCH, HADDINGTON

**Church Street
Haddington
EH41 3EX**

NT 518 739

Scottish Episcopal

www.holytrinitychurch-haddington.co.uk/

Built 1770 on site of original 'Lamp of Lothian'. The present chancel was added and the interior remodelled in neo-Byzantine style in 1930, architect B. N. H. Orphoot. *Stations of the Cross* by Bowman. *Christ Crucified*, Sutherland. Medieval walls of former priory and town defences.

- Sunday: 8.30am, Sung Eucharist 10.00am, Evensong 6.00pm (except July and August); Wednesday: Eucharist 10.00am
- Open Wednesday 10.00am–4.00pm, and in summer Saturday 10.00am–4.00pm or by arrangement (01620 823268)

EAST LOTHIAN

17 **HUMBIE KIRK**

Humbie
EH36 5PA

⚔ NT 461 637

⛪ Church of Scotland

Linked with Bolton Church (4), Saltoun Parish Church (11), Yester Parish Church, Gifford (12)

On banks of Humbie Water, 1.5km (1 mile) north of village

On the site of a pre-Reformation church, set in an oxbow of Humbie Burn, a T-plan Gothic church by James Tod dated 1800. Vestry added 1846, and alterations by David Bryce 1866. Chancel added 1930, probably W. J. Walker Todd. East window by Douglas Strachan. Organ c. 1850, with decorative Gothic dark wood case, from the Norwegian Seamen's Chapel at Granton. Fine gravestones with classical detail dating from earlier church. Two plaques for the united parishes of Humbie and Keith, which have had only 25 ministers since 1590.

- Sunday: 10.00am
- Open daily (01620 810515)

18 **PARISH CHURCH OF ST MICHAEL, INVERESK**

Inveresk
EH21 7UA

⚔ NT 344 721

⛪ Church of Scotland

Off A6124

There has been a church on the site since the 6th century. The present church was built in 1805 to the design of Robert Nisbet; the steeple by William Sibbald. The interior was reorientated and remodelled in 1893 by J. MacIntyre Henry and again in 2002 by Simpson & Brown. Known as the 'Visible Kirk' because of its prominent position, it stands on the site of a Roman praetorium and replaces a medieval church. Fine Adam-style ceiling and some excellent stained glass. Magnificent pipe organ by Lewis 1892, originally built with early form of electric action. Graveyard with many interesting old stones.

- Sunday: 11.15am
- Open by arrangement (0131 665 2689)

19 NORTHESK PARISH CHURCH

**Bridge Street
Musselburgh
EH21 6AA**

⚲ NT 340 727

⛪ Church of Scotland

Opposite Brunton Hall

Opened in 1838, this simple, stone-fronted building was designed by William Burn. Inside, there is an all-round horseshoe gallery under a high vaulted ceiling. Noteworthy are seven stained-glass windows (one by Ballantine & Gardiner, 1892) a First World War memorial plaque, a pink alabaster font and a fine brass eagle lectern. Behind the central pulpit and fronted by a carved pine screen is a recently refurnished Abbot & Smith 2-manual pipe organ of 1904.

- Sunday: 11.00am
- Open on Saturday mornings, 10.00am–12.00 noon February to mid-December, or by arrangement (0131 665 4116)

 (Saturday mornings)

20 ST ANDREW'S HIGH CHURCH, MUSSELBURGH

**70 Millhill
Musselburgh
EH21 7EA**

⚲ NT 345 727

⛪ Church of Scotland

St Andrew's High is the successful voluntary union in 1985 of the previous St Andrew's Church (itself a union of two former UP congregations) and Musselburgh High Church (a former Free congregation). The building was redeveloped and refurbished in 1990–1. The church complex comprises a sanctuary with moveable furniture, reception area, small room and large hall upstairs.

- Sunday: 10.30am
- Open every Saturday 9.00am–12.00 noon (0131 665 7239)

21 ST PETER'S EPISCOPAL, MUSSELBURGH

**High Street
Musselburgh
EH21 7DE**

⚐ NT 348 723

⛪ Scottish Episcopal

🌐 www.stpetersmusselburgh.com

Linked with St Andrew's Episcopal, Prestonpans (33)

Anglican church near the site of the Battle of Pinkie (1547), in a traditional French Gothic style by Paterson & Shiells 1865. Narrow chancel and semi-circular apse and steeply pitched roof. Fine, older stained-glass windows and 17th-century character wooden panelling in St Michael's Chapel. Sundays follow Biblical themes and are friendly, relaxed and relevant. Kids' club during services.

• Sunday: 11.15am; Wednesday: 10.00am
• Open by arrangement (0131 665 2925)

22 OUR LADY OF LORETTO, MUSSELBURGH

**17 Newbigging
Musselburgh
EH21 7RE**

⚐ NT 348 729

⛪ Roman Catholic

Stone building by Archibald Macpherson, opened in 1905. Sanctuary recently modernised. All windows are of stained glass, and the walls of the sanctuary are covered in fine artwork, in gold leaf, depicting the events in the life of our Lord, corresponding to the Joyful Mysteries of the Rosary.

• Saturday: Vigil 6.00pm; Sunday: 9.00am and 11.30am
• Open during daylight hours (0131 665 2137)

23 MUSSELBURGH CONGREGATIONAL CHURCH

**6 Links Street
Musselburgh
EH21 6JL**

⚔ NT 341 729

🏠 Congregational

🌐 www.musselburghcongregational.
org.uk

Behind Brunton Hall

Simple but charming Georgian building completed in 1801, built with stone carried by fishermen and sailors from the shores of the Forth at Fisherrow. Oldest church in Musselburgh and one of the first Congregational churches in Scotland. Pipe organ is a fine example of the work of George Holdich, built 1860 for St Michael's, Appleby. Rebuilt for Musselburgh Congregational Church 1977.

- Sunday: 11.00am
- Open by arrangement (0131 665 5124)

24 ST BALDRED'S CHURCH, NORTH BERWICK

**Dirleton Avenue
North Berwick
EH39 4AY**

⚔ NT 556 853

🏠 Scottish Episcopal

Linked with St Adrian's Church, Gullane (14)

The original Norman-style church by John Henderson 1861 was cleverly extended in 1863 incorporating the old masonry by Seymour & Kinross, who also designed the altar. The porch with its magnificent carved doors was added by Robert Lorimer in 1916. Choir stalls by H. O. Tarbolton, porch doors by Mrs Meredith-Williams. Stained glass by Ballantine & Son.

- Sunday: 11.00am, and 8.00am on 2nd and 4th Sunday of the month
- Open all year, 10.00am–4.00pm (01620 895233)

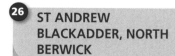

25 ABBEY CHURCH, NORTH BERWICK

High Street
North Berwick
EH39 4HE

NT 551 853
Church of Scotland
www.abbeychurch.co.uk

Linked with Dirleton Kirk (6)

Built 1868 as United Presbyterian by
Robert R. Raeburn in Early English
style. A complete early 20th-century
scheme of stained glass with,
superimposed on one window, an
arrangement of suspended planes
representing an ascent of doves, by
Sax Shaw 1972.

- Sunday: 10.30am and 6.00pm
- Open daylight hours during
  summer months (01620 892800)

26 ST ANDREW BLACKADDER, NORTH BERWICK

High Street
North Berwick
EH39 4HG

NT 553 853
Church of Scotland
www.standrewblackadder.org.uk

The third St Andrew's church in
North Berwick opened in 1883.
Designed by Robert Rowand
Anderson in a Gothic Revival style
with the hall and tower added 1907
by Henry & MacLennan. Important
stained glass by J. Ballantine, Abbey
Studio and William Wilson and a
painting of the second St Andrew's
church in Kirk Ports by W. E. Lockhart.
Organ by Forster & Andrews 1886,
rebuilt and enlarged by Ingram & Co.,
1914. St Andrew's and Blackadder
churches united to form St Andrew
Blackadder in 1988. The sanctuary was
divided horizontally in 2000 to create
meeting rooms.

- Sunday: 9.30am, 10.30am and
  6.00pm; Thursday: 1.00pm
- Open July and August, Monday
  to Saturday 10.00am–4.00pm,
  September to June by arrangement
  (01620 895233)

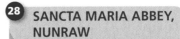

27 OUR LADY STAR OF THE SEA, NORTH BERWICK

**Law Road
North Berwick
EH39 4PN**

NT 553 850

Roman Catholic

www.nbstar.org.uk

Simple Victorian church, 1879, by Dunn & Hansom with seating for 200 people. The chancel was added by Basil Champreys in 1889 and the Lady Chapel by Sir Robert Lorimer in 1901. The interior contains a number of pictures after Benozzo Gozzoli and Botticelli and a Della Robbia (probably a copy).

- Sunday: 9.00am; weekdays: 10.00am
- Open by arrangement (01620 892195)

28 SANCTA MARIA ABBEY, NUNRAW

**Nunraw Abbey
Garvald
EH41 4LW**

NT 593 700

Roman Catholic

www.nunraw.org.uk

1.5km (1 mile) south of Garvald

Modern monastery of Cistercian monks built 1952–70 (but unfinished), architect Peter Whiston. Nunraw house is a historic building and functions as the Abbey guest house, where people may stay for a few days of retreat in the monastic atmosphere.

- Sunday: Mass 11.00am, Vespers 4.00pm, Compline 7.30pm; weekday services: Lauds and Mass 6.45am, Vespers 6.00pm, Compline 7.30pm
- Reception area and Abbey open at all times (01620 830223)

EAST LOTHIAN

EAST LOTHIAN

29 ORMISTON PARISH CHURCH

Main Street
Ormiston
EH35 5HT

🄰 NT 414 693

⛪ Church of Scotland

🌐 www.pencaitlandchurch.org.uk

Linked with Pencaitland Parish Church (30)

The first Presbyterian minister was appointed to Ormiston in 1568. The present Arts and Crafts building, consecrated 1938, was designed by T. Aikman Swan incorporating a cruciform shape and gallery. Carved stone font and wood-panelled pulpit. Three stained-glass windows from the original parish church, depicting Moses, St Paul and the Christ.

- Sunday: 6.30pm
- Open by arrangement (01875 340208)

30 PENCAITLAND PARISH CHURCH

Pencaitland
EH34 5EZ

🄰 NT 443 690

⛪ Church of Scotland

🌐 www.pencaitlandchurch.org.uk

Linked with Ormiston Parish Church (29)

On A6093

Consecrated in 1242, the church has foundations dating from the 12th century. The present building is of the 16th or 17th century and consists of a nave, with a gallery at the west end, and two aisles on the north side, the older called the Winton Aisle and the other the Saltoun Aisle. Churchyard with many interesting gravestones, offering houses, renovated carriage house, stables, harness room and cottage.

- Sunday: 10.30am
- Open by arrangement (01875 340208)

31 CHALMERS MEMORIAL CHURCH, PORT SETON

Gosford Road
Port Seton
EH32 0HG

 NT 403 757

Church of Scotland

www.chalmerschurch.co.uk

Built to a design by Sydney Mitchell for the United Free Church; foundation stone laid in 1904. An excellent example of Arts and Crafts design, it has a very elegant spire and bell-tower and unique stencilled interior. Stained-glass windows by Margaret Chilton and Marjorie Kemp 1924–50.

- Sunday: 10.15am and 11.10am all year, and 6.15pm in winter
- Open by arrangement (01875 812481)

32 PRESTONKIRK

Traprain Parish, St Baldred

Preston Road
East Linton
EH40 3DS

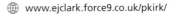 NT 592 778

Church of Scotland

www.ejclark.force9.co.uk/pkirk/

Linked with Stenton (35), Whittingehame (39)

Dedicated to St Baldred. The former chancel is the best fragment of 13th-century church architecture in East Lothian. The tower dates from 1631; the main building from 1770, enlarged 1824, redesigned internally 1892 by James Jerdan and refurbished 2004. Organ by Vincent of Sutherland overhauled 2004. St Baldred window and two Second World War memorial windows by William Wilson. Follow signs to Preston Mill.

- Sunday: 11.00am
- Open by arrangement (01620 860227)

 (in halls)

 (by arrangement)

EAST LOTHIAN

33 ST ANDREW'S EPISCOPAL, PRESTONPANS

**West Loan
Prestonpans
EH32 9AN**

NT 392 749

Scottish Episcopal

www.stpetersmusselburgh.com

Linked with St Peter's Episcopal, Musselburgh (21)

Stone-built simple hall-church, built as a Free Kirk in 1843, with slender cast-iron columns supporting the roof. Light, spacious interior. Former gallery now enclosed to form upper room over kitchen and toilets. Fine stained glass including a recent window by Sax Shaw.

• Sunday: 9.30am and 11.15am
• Open by arrangement (0131 665 2925)

 34 SPOTT PARISH CHURCH

**Spott
EH42 1RJ**

NT 674 756

Church of Scotland

www.belhavenparishchurch.org.uk

Linked with Belhaven Parish Church (3)

In middle of village, 3km (2 miles) south of Dunbar

A little T-plan harled kirk of 1790 and 1809, incorporating the 17th-century Hay Aisle. The old jougs are hung outside the east door, dating from the 17th century, when witch-burning was recorded in the church records. Simple box pews and an elaborate pulpit with Corinthian columns supporting the sounding board.

• Sunday: 10.00am
• Open by arrangement (01368 863098)

35 STENTON PARISH CHURCH

Traprain Parish

**Main Street
Stenton
EH42 1TD**

⚲ NT 623 743

⛪ Church of Scotland

🌐 www.ejclark.force9.co.uk/pkirk/

Linked with Prestonkirk (32), Whittingehame Parish Church (39)

On B6370 between Gifford and Dunbar

By William Burn, 1829, a T-plan kirk with a splendid east tower. Redesigned internally by James Jerdan, 1892. Stained glass by E. C. Kempe and Ballantine & Gardiner. In the graveyard is a fragment of the 16th-century kirk and a fine selection of monuments. Rood well in village.

- Sunday: 9.30am
- Open by arrangement (01620 860227)

Ⓑ 〰

36 ST MARTIN OF TOURS, TRANENT

**High Street
Tranent
EH33 1HJ**

⚲ NT 410 727

⛪ Roman Catholic

East end of High Street

This is the third church building on the site in 100 years and was built in 1969 in an octagonal shape using a Scandinavian compressed-timber girder design. Contains two rough stained-glass windows and an early 20th-century Italian crucifix above the altar. Irish limestone statue of classical design of St Martin as a Roman soldier and an original icon of St Martin in Orthodox style.

- Saturday: Vigil 6.00pm; Sunday: Mass 10.30am; Tuesday to Friday: 9.00am
- Open by arrangement (01875 610232)

37 TRANENT METHODIST CHURCH

**Tranent Day Centre
3 Church Street
Tranent
EH33 1AA**

 NT 405 728

 Methodist

🌐 www.edinburghandforth

methodistcircuit.org.uk

Linked with Cockenzie Methodist Church (5), Dunbar Methodist Church (10)

The Methodist congregation of Tranent now worships in Tranent Day Centre and remains rooted in its distinctive traditional community. The Day Centre also hosts many youth and community groups.

- Sunday: 11.00am
- Open daily (0131 221 9029)

---

38 ST MARY'S PARISH CHURCH, WHITEKIRK

**Whitekirk
EH42 1XS**

 NT 596 815

 Church of Scotland

Linked with Athelstaneford Parish Church (2)

On A198, 8km (5 miles) south-east of North Berwick

Dating from the 12th century, the original building was reconstructed during the 15th century starting with the vaulted stone choir, built in 1439 by Adam Hepburn of Hailes. In medieval times, Whitekirk was an important place of pilgrimage. The church was set on fire in 1914 by suffragettes. Restored by Robert Lorimer. Ceiled wagon roof over nave and transepts, communion table, pulpit, lectern and font all by Lorimer. Stained glass by C. E. Kempe 1889 and Karl Parsons 1916. Tithe barn and historic graveyard.

- Sunday: 11.30am
- Open daily (01620 890410)

39 WHITTINGEHAME PARISH CHURCH

Traprain Parish

**Whittingehame
EH41 4QA**

⚐ NT 603 737

⛪ Church of Scotland

🌐 www.ejclark.force9.co.uk/pkirk/

Linked with Prestonkirk (32),
Stenton Parish Church (35)

On B6370 between Gifford and
Dunbar

Spiky battlemented Gothic T-plan
church built 1722, and added to by
Barclay & Lamb in 1820 for James
Balfour, grandfather of A. J. Balfour,
Prime Minister 1902–5. Eighteenth-
century burial enclosure of Buchan
Sydserfs of Ruchlaw and good late
17th-century headstones show that
there was an earlier church on the
site.

• Occasional services
• Open by arrangement (01620
860227)

40 ABBEY ST BATHANS PARISH CHURCH

Langton and Lammermuir
Kirk

**Abbey St Bathans
TD11 3TX**

⚐ NT 758 623

⛪ Church of Scotland

Linked with Cranshaws Kirk (48),
Langton Parish Church, Gavinton
(54), Longformacus Parish Church
(61)

5km (3 miles) off B6355

Continuing many centuries of
Christian worship on the site in a
secluded valley and conveying a great
sense of peace, the present church
dates from 1858, in a Romanesque
Revival style by John Lessels. The
north and east walls contain parts
of an earlier building; a stone effigy
of a prioress is displayed in a niche
in the east wall. Recently updated
information leaflets for adults, and
worksheet for children.

• Every 3rd Sunday at 11.45am
• Open daily (01361 882728)

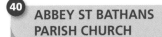

41 AYTON PARISH CHURCH

Ayton
TD14 5RH

NT 927 609

Church of Scotland

Linked with Burnmouth Parish Church (42), Foulden and Mordington Parish Church (53), Reston Parish Church (64)

South side of village, opposite road to Chirnside

First-pointed Gothic-style building with 36m (118ft) spire designed by James Maitland Wardrop 1864–6. High-quality stained glass by Ballantine & Sons. Fine organ by Forster & Andrews of Hull 1894, restored by James Lightoller of Berwick 1997. Occasional organ recitals. In the burial ground are the ivy-clad ruins of the 12th-century St Dionysius's church.

- Sunday: 11.00am on 1st and 3rd Sunday of the month
- Open by arrangement (01890 781333)

42 BURNMOUTH PARISH CHURCH

Burnmouth
TD14 5SP

NT 956 610

Church of Scotland

Linked with Ayton Parish Church (41), Foulden and Mordington Parish Church (53), Reston Parish Church (64)

'Halfway doon the Brae'

The church is built on the cliff side and is entered from a door in the rear. A plain hall-church of 1888, refurbished 1929. The pews are originally from Dunblane Cathedral. In the building is a memorial to the men of Burnmouth who lost their lives in the east-coast fishing disaster of 'Black Friday', 14 October 1881.

- Sunday: 9.45am on 2nd and 4th Sunday of the month
- Open by arrangement (01890 781333)

WC

43 **CHANNELKIRK PARISH CHURCH**

Channelkirk
TD2 6PT

NT 481 545

Church of Scotland

www.clchurch.org.uk

Linked with Lauder Old Church (58)

3km (2 miles) west of Oxton

Commanding a fine view down the valley, this is a historic site dating back to St Cuthbert; the Mother Kirk of Lauderdale, established by Dryburgh Abbey. Present building erected 1817 by James Gillespie Graham in Perpendicular Gothic. Original pulpit and fittings. Bell of 1702 still rung each Sunday.

- Sunday: 10.00am March to October. November to February: services are in War Memorial Hall, Oxton
- Open daily (01578 722220)

44 **CHIRNSIDE PARISH CHURCH**

Kirk Hill
Chirnside
TD11 3XH

NT 869 561

Church of Scotland

Linked with Edrom Parish Church (51), Bonkyl Parish Church, Preston (63)

South side of village at junction of A6105 and B6237

The chevron-patterned Norman doorway at the south-west corner of the church dates from the 12th century. The church was largely rebuilt in 1878 with the church hall, vestry and tower added in 1905–7. Buried in the kirkyard are the famous 17th-century Reforming minister, Henry Erskine, and the 1960s Formula 1 world champion, Jim Clark.

- Sunday: 11.00am
- Open by arrangement (01890 819109)

B

SCOTTISH BORDERS

BERWICKSHIRE

45 THE PRIORY CHURCH, COLDINGHAM

Coldingham
TD14 5PY

NT 904 659

Church of Scotland

www.stebba-coldinghampriory.org.uk

Influential centre of Christian witness in the Scottish Borders since the 7th century. Successor to nearby St Aebbe's Monastery, attached to Durham Cathedral for 300 years. Present church formed from choir and sanctuary area which comprised eastern arm of early 13th-century cruciform-plan Priory Church of St Mary. Splendid free-standing restored arch of original church to west of main building. South and west walls rebuilt 1662, and extensive renovation in 1850s. Interior renovation 1950 providing present chancel and its furnishings. Nine modern stained-glass windows. Detailed scale model of the Priory is on exhibition.

- Sunday: 10.00am
- Open Wednesday, May to September 2.00–4.00pm; Sunday 2.00–4.00pm July and August or by arrangement (01890 77182)

46 COLDSTREAM PARISH CHURCH

High Street
Coldstream
TD12 4AG

NT 844 400

Church of Scotland

Linked with Eccles Parish Church (50)

The square church tower is a distinctive feature. The tower and the west entrance are part of the original church built 1718. The rest of the church was rebuilt in 1905 to a design by J. M. Dick Peddie. A classical nave-and-aisles church with a fine stone pulpit. The church contains many reminders of its and the town's close association with the Coldstream Guards. The king's and regimental colours hang in the chancel. Plaque to Rev. Adam Thomson who formed the Coldstream Free Bible Press in 1845, thus breaking the monopoly held by Oxford and Cambridge Universities and the king's printers in Scotland.

- Sunday: 11.15am
- Open June to August, Thursday 2.00–4.00pm or by arrangement (01890 883149)

B ♿ WC 👂 📖

47 ST MARY'S AND ALL SOULS, COLDSTREAM

**Lennel Road
Coldstream
TD12 4EP**

🏛 NT 846 402

⛪ Scottish Episcopal

🌐 http://stmaryandstandrew.org.uk

Linked with St Andrew's Church, Kelso (106)

There was a corrugated-iron church on the site when the congregation split from being a mission church of Christ Church, Duns. The present building, by Charles T. Ewing, came into use in 1914. Two windows in the sanctuary were given by the Sunday School. Painted decoration in the apse by Mrs Ellington. The pews, altar, hangings, priest's vestments and some other items came from the old chapel at The Hirsel.

- Sunday: 8.30am and 10.30am; Thursday: 10.30am
- Open by arrangement (01573 224163)

48 CRANSHAWS KIRK

Langton and Lammermuir Kirk

**Cranshaws
TD11 3SJ**

🏛 NT 692 618

⛪ Church of Scotland

Linked with Abbey St Bathans Parish Church (40), Langton Parish Church, Gavinton (54), Longformacus Parish Church (61)

On B6355 between Duns and Gifford

First mentioned in 1275, possibly dedicated to St Ninian, the 1739 church was rebuilt 1899 by architect George Fortune in Romanesque Revival style. Contains royal coat-of-arms of 1471–1500, installed opposite the pulpit by James VI (1566–1625), who once attended – and the minister omitted prayers for the monarch. Recently updated information leaflets for adults, and worksheet for children.

- Every 3rd Sunday at 11.45am
- Open daily (01361 882728)

49 CHRIST CHURCH, DUNS

Teindhall Green
Duns
TD11 3DX

NT 787 543

Scottish Episcopal

www.edinburgh.anglican.org

Off Preston Road (A6112)

Built 1854; design, suggested by Col. William Hay of Duns Castle, based on a small Lutheran church in the Rhine Valley, Germany. Romanesque style with aisles and a tower with broach spire. Very good organ by Harrison & Harrison. One of the windows is a memorial to the late Admiral Sir Bertram and Lady Ramsay; the Admiral was Commander-in-Chief at the Dunkirk evacuation in 1940 and allied Naval Commander-in-Chief at the Normandy invasion in 1944.

- 8.30am on 2nd and 4th Sunday of the month; 10.30am on 1st, 3rd and 5th Sunday
- Open during daylight hours (01361 882209)

50 ECCLES PARISH CHURCH

Eccles
TD5 7QS

NT 764 413

Church of Scotland

Linked with Coldstream Parish Church (46)

Near centre of village, on road to Birgham

First documented in 1156, dedicated to St Mary; rededicated to St Andrew in 1248. Following the dissolution of the monasteries, stored corn burned in 1543; in 1544 the church was assaulted and 80 people slain; in 1545 Hecles Abbey was one of the places 'brent, rased and cast downe'. The oldest surviving relic is a bell dated 1659. The present church was built in 1774 with seating for 1,000 people, before major internal renovations in 1930. The building is a large hall-church with round-headed and circular windows. A square tower with octagonal belfry rises above the main entrance. War Memorial window of 1948 by Douglas McLundie of Abbey Studios.

- Sunday: 9.45am
- Open by arrangement (01890 840240)

51 EDROM PARISH CHURCH

Edrom
TD11 3PX

⚔ NT 826 558

⛪ Church of Scotland

Linked with Chirnside Parish Church (44), Bonkyl Parish Church, Preston (63)

Off A6105

The 15th-century Blackadder Aisle, under the care of Historic Scotland, was built by Robert Blackadder, Archbishop of Glasgow, in 1499. The T-plan kirk had major alterations in 1886 including the open-timber scissor roof. The Edrom Arch (also Historic Scotland) was the entrance to the 12th-century kirk and is now a burial vault. Information plaques on site.

- 9.45am on 2nd and 4th Sunday of the month
- Open by arrangement (01890 819109)

52 FOGO KIRK

Fogo
TD11 3RA

⚔ NT 773 492

⛪ Church of Scotland

Linked with Ladykirk (57), Leitholm Church (60), Swinton Kirk (65), Whitsome Kirk (67)

6.5km (4 miles) north-east of Greenlaw, off B6460

This peaceful spot has church remnants from 900 years ago. In the vestry is one of the oldest gravestones in Berwickshire. Two laird's lofts, entered by outside stairs, have coats-of-arms (1670s) of the Hoggs and the Trotters. These, the box pews and the small plain-glass windows make Fogo Kirk unique. The lychgate is the War Memorial; and 16 war graves from the Second World War are in the kirkyard.

- 11.15am every 3rd Sunday
- Open during daylight hours (01890 860228)

53 FOULDEN AND MORDINGTON PARISH CHURCH

**Main Street
Foulden
TD15 1UH**

NT 931 558

Church of Scotland

Linked with Ayton Parish Church (41), Burnmouth Parish Church (42), Reston Parish Church (64)

On main street (A6105)

Since the 12th century, the site has been associated with Coldingham Priory, 1176. The present building dates from 1786 and is sited slightly to the north of the original. A simple rectangular church with Gothic windows and a gabled belfry. The interior has Tudor Gothic detailing. Medieval font. The kirk bell dates from 1704 and was made by John Meikle of Edinburgh. In 1586, commissioners of James VI met those of Elizabeth of England in the church to receive a letter professing her innocence in the death of Mary Queen of Scots.

- Sunday: 11.30am
- Open by arrangement (01890 781333)

54 LANGTON PARISH CHURCH, GAVINTON

Langton and Lammermuir Kirk

**Gavinton
TD11 3QT**

NT 767 522

Church of Scotland

Linked with Abbey St Bathans Parish Church (40), Cranshaws Kirk (48), Longformacus Parish Church (61)

Off A6105, 3km (2 miles) west of Duns

The present church of 1872 replaced an earlier building of 1798 and dominates the village. Gothic in style, with a steeple topped with the 1798 weathercock. Display of the mort bell, communion tokens and the coat-of-arms of the minesweeper HMS *Gavinton*. Allen organ of 2005. Recently updated information leaflets for adults, and worksheets for children.

- Sunday: 10.00am
- Open by arrangement (01361 882728)

55 ST MICHAEL'S, GORDON

**Manse Road
Gordon
TD3 6LS**

NT 645 432

Church of Scotland

Linked with Greenlaw Church (56), Legerwood Parish Church (59), Westruther Parish Church (66)

The original 12th-century church was replaced by a new building in 1763, heightened and extended in 1897 by Dunn & Findlay.The only thing remaining of the early church is the bell, founded in 1714 by one Robert Maxwell! Three-light stained glass window of 1940. Pipe organ, 1895 Forster & Andrews, moved from East Linton and rebuilt by David Stark, 2000.

- 10.45am on 1st, 3rd and 5th Sunday of the month
- Open by arrangement (01361 810316)

56 GREENLAW CHURCH

**Church Street
Greenlaw
TD10 6YE**

NT 712 462

Church of Scotland

Linked with St Michaels, Gordon (55), Legerwood Parish Church (59), Westruther Parish Church (66)

There has been a church on the site since before 1147. The present church was built 1675 and lengthened 1712. The east and west lofts were erected 1721 and the north loft 1784. A prison, resembling a church tower, was added by 1712 and was in use until 1824. The tower houses the town clock and church bell, provided by Thomas Broomfield c. 1696 and recast 1726.

- Sunday: 9.45am
- Open Saturday 10.00am–12 noon or by arrangement (01361 810253)

SCOTTISH BORDERS

BERWICKSHIRE

57 LADYKIRK

**Ladykirk
TD15 1XL**

⟁ NT 889 477

⛪ Church of Scotland

Linked with Fogo Kirk (52),
Leithholm Church (60), Swinton
Kirk (65), Whitsome Kirk (67)

6.5km (4 miles) east of Swinton, off
B6470

Built in 1500 by James IV to 'Our
Lady' with an all-stone construction
including the unique stone roof,
to withstand 'fire and flood'. The
Scottish and English Wardens of
the East March met regularly in the
parish; the last peace treaty between
Scotland and England was signed in
Ladykirk in 1560. Many stained-glass
windows; the wooden pews and
pipe organ were installed in the 20th
century.

- 11.15am on 2nd and 4th Sunday of
  the month
- Open during daylight hours (01890
  860228)

58 LAUDER OLD CHURCH

**Market Place
Lauder
TD2 6SR**

⟁ NT 531 475

⛪ Church of Scotland

🌐 www.clchurch.org.uk

Linked with Channelkirk Parish
Church (43)

Built 1673 by Sir William Bruce, in the
shape of a Greek cross with four equal
arms and a central octagonal bell-
tower. Various alterations were made
through the 18th and 19th centuries.
The porches were added later.
Splendid pulpit with sounding board.
Walled graveyard with watchtower of
1830. Pulpit of 1820.

- Sunday: 11.30am
- Open 9.00am–6.00pm daily (01578
  722220)

Aberlady Parish Church 1

Belhaven Parish Church, Dunbar 3

Bolton Parish Church 4

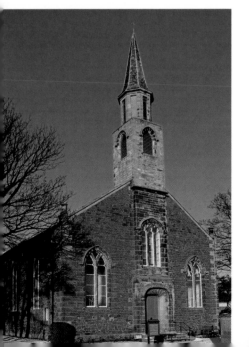

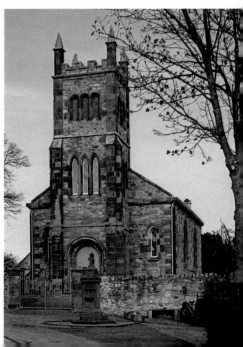

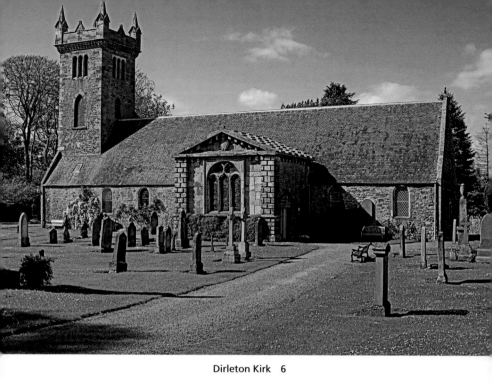

Dirleton Kirk   6

Our Lady of the Waves, Dunbar   9

Saltoun Parish Church, East Saltoun   11

Bowden Kirk 87

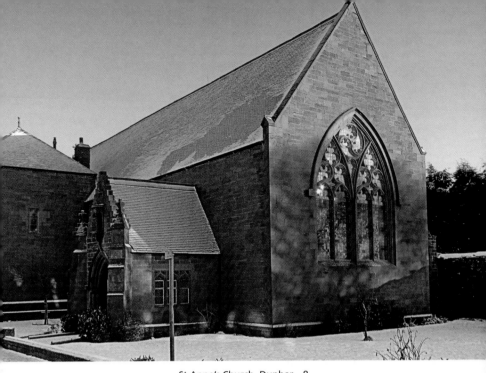

St Anne's Church, Dunbar   8

Chalmers Memorial Church, Port Seton   31

St Mary's Parish Church, Whitekirk   38

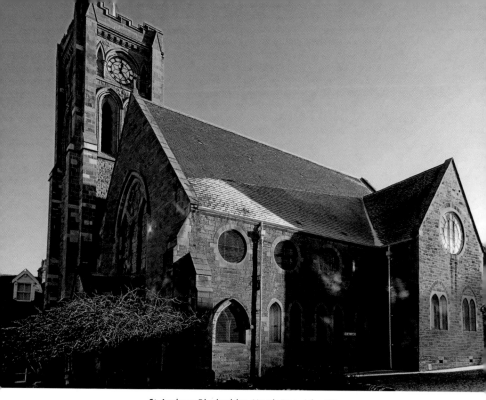

St Andrew Blackadder, North Berwick   26

Drumelzier Kirk   69

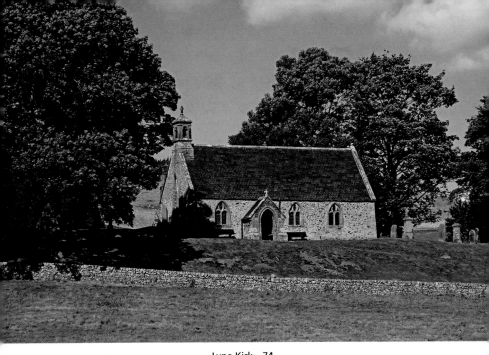

Lyne Kirk   74

Stobo Kirk   80

Kelso Old Parish Church   104

Yester Parish Church, Gifford   12

59 LEGERWOOD PARISH CHURCH

**Kirk Hill
Legerwood
TD4 6AT**

NT 594 434

Church of Scotland

Linked with St Michael's, Gordon (55), Greenlaw Church (56), Westruther Parish Church (66)

The church dates from 1127 and is one of the most complete Romanesque churches in the Borders. Repaired in 1717 and 1804. Chancel restored in 1898 (Hardy & Wight); fine Norman arch and many other historic features. Stained glass by Ballantine & Gardiner.

- 11.45am on 1st Sunday of the month
- Open daily (01361 810316)

60 LEITHOLM CHURCH

**Leitholm
TD12 4JN**

NT 791 441

Church of Scotland

Linked with Fogo Kirk (52), Ladykirk (57), Swinton Kirk (65), Whitsome Kirk (67)

50 metres up lane on south side of Leitholm village

There was no permanent church in Leitholm until 1835, when the present church was opened as a relief church. In 1951, a new pulpit, font, communion table and pipe organ were donated, and new pews in 1968. The clock in the gallery is in memory of three young boys who were tragically drowned during the annual trip to Spittal in 1966.

- 9.45am on 2nd and 4th Sunday of the month
- Open by arrangement (01890 860228)

61 LONGFORMACUS PARISH CHURCH

Langton and Lammermuir Kirk

**Longformacus
TD11 3PE**

NT 694 572

Church of Scotland

Linked with Abbey St Bathans Parish Church (40), Cranshaws Kirk (48), Langton Parish Church, Gavinton (54)

Off B6355, Gifford-to-Duns road

There has been a church on this site on the south side of Dye Water since 1243. Extensively rebuilt from a ruinous state in 1730, repaired 1830 and renovated 1892 by George Fortune. Stained glass by Marjorie Kemp and G. J. Baguley, including windows in memory of the Brown family of Longformacus and the Smiths of Whitchester. Recently updated information leaflets for children and worksheets for children.

- Every 3rd Sunday at 11.45am
- Open daily (01361 882728)

62 MERTOUN PARISH CHURCH

**Mertoun
TD6 0EA**

NT 615 318

Church of Scotland

Linked with Maxton Parish Church (114), Newtown Church (121), St Boswells Parish Church (128)

1.5km (1 mile) south of B6404

The original church of 1241, not on this site, was dedicated to St Ninian. The present church was built 1652, renovated 1820 and enlarged 1898 with the addition of the north aisle and vestry. On the outside of the south wall, the remains of a set of jougs can be seen. Birdcage belfry, bell dated 1707, sundial on south-east corner. Rose window in west gable.

- Sunday: 11.45am on 1st and 3rd Sunday of the month; 5th Sunday: service in rotation with Maxton, Newtown and St Boswells
- Open by arrangement (01835 822355)

63 BONKYL PARISH CHURCH, PRESTON

Bonkyl
Preston
TD11 3RJ

⚔ NT 808 596

⛪ Church of Scotland

Linked with Chirnside Parish Church (44), Edrom Parish Church (51)

5km (3 miles) north of Preston, off B6438

Bonkyl (also spelled Bunkle or Bonkle) is a rectangular church with Romanesque features built in 1820 with some later insertions. The Old Kirk, of which a semi-circular domed stone-slab apse survives (to south-east of church) was one of the earliest examples of medieval ecclesiastical architecture in Scotland (late 11th century). In nearby Preston is another ruin, Preston Old Kirk, 12th century, its walls having survived because of their conversion to family burial vaults.

- 9.45am on 1st and 3rd Sunday of the month
- Open by arrangement (01890 819109)

64 RESTON PARISH CHURCH

Main Street
Reston
TD14 5LD

⚔ NT 787 621

⛪ Church of Scotland

Linked with Ayton Parish Church (41), Burnmouth Parish Church (42), Foulden and Mordington Parish Church (53)

South side of main street in centre of village (B6438)

Built in 1879, originally the building was a Free Church of Scotland. A simple rectangular building in Early Gothic style with a bellcote. The retention of the box pews is unusual.

- 11.00am on 1st and 3rd Sunday of the month. On the 1st and 4th Sunday, there is a service in Grantshouse Village Hall.
- Open by arrangement (01890 781333)

65 **SWINTON KIRK**

**Swinton
TD11 3JJ**

NT 839 476

Church of Scotland

Linked with Fogo Kirk (52), Ladykirk (57), Leithholm Church (60), Whitsome Kirk (67)

East end of Swinton village

Swinton Kirk has been greatly altered, but the south and east walls are 1,000 years old and the aumbry can still be seen. The last renovation (1910) was by Robert Lorimer. The 1499 bell was rung as a death knell after Flodden (1513). Behind the communion table is an effigy of Alan Swinton (1200), while the oldest stone coat-of-arms in Britain (the Swintons') is above the gallery door. The windows are made of squares of ancient glass.

- 11.15am on 1st and 5th Sunday of the month
- Open during daylight hours (01890 860228)

66 **WESTRUTHER PARISH CHURCH**

**Westruther
TD3 6NE**

NT 634 500

Church of Scotland

Linked with St Michaels, Gordon (55), Greenlaw Church (56), Legerwood Parish Church (59)

In centre of village, on B6456

The present church, 1840 by John Smith, was built alongside the earlier church, 1649, now a ruin. A plain box of whin with sandstone rubble walls. A carved wooden font of 1908 incorporates a stone font from Bassendean Chapel and the pewter bowl from the old church. Arts and Crafts stained-glass windows of 1896 and 1900 and a modern window of 1966.

- 11.45am on 2nd and 4th Sunday of the month
- Open by arrangement (01578 740655)

67 WHITSOME KIRK

**Whitsome
TD11 3NB**

NT 861 505

Church of Scotland

Linked with Fogo Kirk (52), Ladykirk (57), Leithholm Church (60), Swinton Kirk (65)

West end of Whitsome village

There are no remains of the old Whitsome Kirk, which was in the middle of the graveyard. The present kirk (1803) had a gallery round three sides with the pulpit on the south wall. The seating arrangement was altered in 1912 when the chancel was added. Font, 1910, by Robert Lorimer.

- 9.45am on 1st and 3rd Sunday of the month
- Open during daylight hours (01890 860228)

68 BROUGHTON, GLENHOLM AND KILBUCHO PARISH CHURCH

**Calzeat
Broughton
ML12 6HQ**

NT 111 368

Church of Scotland

www.uppertweeddale.org.uk/broughton_kirk_9.html

Linked with Drumelzier Kirk (69), Skirling Parish Church (79), Stobo Kirk (80), Tweedsmuir Kirk (83)

By Biggar

Built in 1804 and extended in 1886 by Robert Bryden of Broughton and Glasgow, to whom there is a memorial stained-glass window in the north wall. The most recent of many changes to the building over the years have been the provision of a door for access for disabled, rearrangement of some pews to provide a gathering area, the installation of a fine organ (from local fund-raising), and a new lighting system.

- Sunday: 10.00am
- Open by arrangement (01899 830366)

69 DRUMELZIER KIRK

**Drumelzier
ML12 6JD**

⚐ NT 135 343

🏛 Church of Scotland

🌐 www.uppertweeddale.org.uk/
stobo_and_drumelzier_5.html

Linked with Broughton, Glenholm
and Kilbucho Parish Church (68),
Skirling Parish Church (79), Stobo
Kirk (80), Tweedsmuir Kirk (83)

By Broughton off B712

A simple rectangular building of pre-
Reformation origins. The original
date is uncertain, but it owes its
present appearance largely to major
alterations carried out in 1872 (John
Mitchell, architect). Bellcote, 17th
century, on the west gable. Burial
vault 1617 for the Tweedies of
Drumelzier.

- Occasional services
- Open during daylight hours (01721
  720568)

70 EDDLESTON PARISH CHURCH

**Bellfield Road
Eddleston
EH45 8QP**

⚐ NT 244 472

🏛 Church of Scotland

Linked with Peebles Old Parish
Church (75)

The site has been in continuous
occupation since the 12th century, the
present building being erected in 1829
incorporating a number of carved
stones of the 17th and 18th centuries.
The church was rebuilt after a fire
in 1897 and the vestry and chancel
added. The restoration was paid for
by the then Lord Elibank, and Mr
Somerville of Portmore. The church
bell, one of the oldest in the country,
was cast in 1507. The 2-manual pedal
organ of 1907 from St Blane's in
Dunblane was rebuilt here in 1980.

- Sunday: 11.45am except 5th Sunday
  6.00pm; Thursday: 7.00pm
- Open by arrangement (01721 720568)

71 INNERLEITHEN CHURCH

**93 Leithen Road
Innerleithen
EH44 6HN**

NT 332 369

Church of Scotland

www.itwcos.org

Linked with Traquair Kirk (81)

Built between 1864 and 1867, the church is the work of Frederick Thomas Pilkington. Its most striking features are the beautiful east elevation, the minaret windows and the elaborate carving. The chancel was added by J. McIntyre Henry in 1889. Stained-glass windows by Ballantine & Son, 2-manual pipe organ by Brook & Co., 1892. On a plinth in front of the church stands part of the shaft of a 9th-century decorated cross, discovered in the foundations of the earlier church.

• Sunday: 11.30am
• Open by arrangement (01896 830309)

72 ST ANDREW'S, INNERLEITHEN

**Church Street
Innerleithen
EH44 3JA**

NT 333 371

Scottish Episcopal

www.stpeterspeebles.org.uk

Linked with St Peter's Church, Peebles (77)

A small yet beautiful church by C. E. Howse, dedicated in 1904. The altar screen attractively separates the nave and sanctuary. A mural behind the altar depicts the *Visitation of the Shepherds*, painted in the style of Phoebe Traquair by William Blacklock of Edinburgh. Two stained-glass windows either side of the sanctuary, in memory of Capt. R. M. B. Welsh, depict St George and the Dragon. A window in the nave, in memory of Mrs F. Ballantyne, illustrates the hymn *All things bright and beautiful*, with local scenery, flora, animals and birds.

• Sunday: 10.00am
• Open Thursdays by arrangement (01721 720571)

73 ST JAMES'S, INNERLEITHEN

**High Street
Innerleithen
EH44 6HD**

NT 329 366

Roman Catholic

Linked with St Joseph's Church, Peebles (78)

Built in 1881 to a design by John Biggar; some interesting works of art including a large icon of Our Lady of Częstochowa, Poland. This is by K. Kryska 1944, the captain of Polish Forces based in Peeblesshire. Other monuments include ones dating from 1861 and a copy of the bust of John Ogilvie. The sanctuary has been brought back into use, and a narthex has been built inside the church to provide toilet and kitchen facilities. A rood-screen division within the church provides a gathering and social space towards the rear of the nave.

- Sunday: 11.30am
- Open summer 10.00am–4.00pm (times may vary) or by arrangement (01721 720865)

74 LYNE KIRK

**Lyne
EH45 8NS**

NT 192 405

Church of Scotland

Linked with Manor Kirk (110)

On A72 from Peebles

Located on the site of a 12th-century church, the present church was built between 1640 and 1645 by John Hay of Yester (later 1st Earl of Tweeddale). The porch was added in the 19th century. The church retains its 17th-century interior, and of particular interest are the Dutch pulpit and canopied pews dated 1644. Pre-Reformation font. The earliest stone in the graveyard is dated 1707; the Adam and Eve stone, dated 1712, is uncommon. Roman fort of Lyne immediately to the west.

- 11.00am on 1st Sunday of the month
- Open daily (01721 721749)

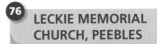

75 PEEBLES OLD PARISH CHURCH

**High Street
Peebles
EH45 8SW**

⋏ NT 246 406

🏠 Church of Scotland

🌐 www.topcop.org.uk

Linked with Eddleston Parish Church (70)

Built 1887 by William Young of London in Gothic style containing features from earlier church. Fine Crown spire dominates the High Street. An inviting flight of steps leads up to the entrance. The chancel was reconstructed by J. D. Cairns 1937. Entrance screen of 1965, woodwork by Scott Morton, metalwork by Charles Henshaw & Son. Stained glass by Helen Turner, Daniel Cottier and Crear McCartney. Pulpit 1913 by Peter MacGregor Chalmers. Part of pre-Reformation font incorporated in table in crossing, by Mitchall Design 1998. Pipe organ by August Gern 1887, extensively rebuilt.

- Sunday: 10.00am; Monday to Saturday: 10.00am
- Open 10.00am–4.00pm all year (01721 723986)

76 LECKIE MEMORIAL CHURCH, PEEBLES

**Church of Scotland
St Andrew's Leckie Parish**

**Eastgate
Peebles
EH45 8AD**

⋏ NT 253 404

🏠 Church of Scotland

🌐 www.standrewsleckie.co.uk

Handsome Gothic-style church with a fine terraced situation, built 1875-7 to designs by Peddie & Kinnear in memory of Thomas Leckie, the first pastor of the Associate Burgher Congregation from 1794 to 1821. Gifted in trust by the surviving members of his family. Following union in 1976 with St Andrew's Church, now home of the St Andrew's Leckie congregation. The pews have been removed and replaced with removable seating, so the building is now multi-functional.

- Sunday: 10.30am and 6.00pm
- Open by arrangement (01721 723121)

77 **ST PETER'S CHURCH, PEEBLES**

Eastgate
Peebles
EH45 8AD

⚐ NT 253 405

⛪ Scottish Episcopal

🌐 www.stpeterspeebles.org.uk

Linked with St Andrew's, Innerleithen (72)

Designed by William Burn and built 1836–7 in finely hewn ashlar with an open timber roof. The chancel was added 1884 by Hay & Henderson. The floor is paved with mosaic tiles, as is the reredos, beautifully executed with devices in gold and colour. Choir seats and altar of oak. Piscina on the south side with stone shelf and foliated basin. Fine stained glass. The organ, 1909, by Harrison, is one of the smallest 3-manual instruments ever built and has been praised for its compactness and excellence of tone.

- Sunday: Holy Communion 8.30am, Eucharist 10.30am; Thursday: Holy Communion 10.00am
- Open 9.00am–5.00pm, or daylight hours (01721 720571)

78 **ST JOSEPH'S CHURCH, PEEBLES**

Rosetta Road
Peebles
EH45 8JU

⚐ NT 248 407

⛪ Roman Catholic

Linked with St James's, Innerleithen (73)

The present building was opened in 1858. The interior was reordered in 1971. The church includes various stained-glass windows and statues. The most significant is the recently restored 14 *Stations of the Cross* by the Alinari Brothers of Florence. Reredos with marble veneers by Reginald Fairlie.

- Saturday: Vigil 6.00pm; Sunday: 9.30am
- Open daily, 9.00am–6.00pm (01721 720865)

B

79 SKIRLING PARISH CHURCH

**Skirling
ML12 6HD**

⚐ NT 075 390

🏛 Church of Scotland

🌐 www.uppertweeddale.org.uk/
skirling_kirk_4.html

Linked with Broughton (68), Drumelzier (69), Stobo (80), Tweedsmuir (83)

3km (2 miles) east of Biggar on A72

The earliest reference to a church is in 1275. The church was virtually rebuilt in 1720 with significant alterations in 1891. The bellcote is of particular interest, as is the sundial on the tower. Communion table and matching chairs were presented by the artist, Sir D. Y. Cameron, in 1948. Round churchyard enclosed by a ha-ha and entered through fine wrought-iron gates.

- Sunday: 11.30am
- Open by arrangement (01899 860295)

  (by arrangement)

80 STOBO KIRK

**Stobo
EH45 8NX**

⚐ NT 183 377

🏛 Church of Scotland

🌐 www.uppertweeddale.org.uk/
stobo_and_drumelzier_5.html

Linked with Broughton (68), Drumelzier (69), Skirling (79), Tweedsmuir (83)

B712, off A72, 6.5km (4 miles) west of Peebles

One of the oldest churches in the Borders, and standing on the site of a 6th-century church reputedly founded by St Kentigern (St Mungo). Comprising nave, sanctuary and tower, the latter rebuilt from first-floor level, probably 16th century. Major restoration 1863, John Lessels. North-aisle chapel restored 1929, James Grieve. A new stone floor laid and a meeting room formed at first-floor level of the tower 1991.

- Sunday: 11.30am
- Open during daylight hours (01721 720568)

SCOTTISH BORDERS

PEEBLESSHIRE

81 TRAQUAIR KIRK

**Kirkhouse
Traquair
EH44 6PU**

Å NT 320 335

⌂ Church of Scotland

⊕ www.itwcos.org

Linked with Innerleithen Church (71)

1.5km (1 mile) south of Traquair village

There has been a church at Traquair since the early 12th century. The present simple, elegant country church is dated 1778 and has a traditional plan with a central pulpit. Comprehensive restoration completed 2001. A monument on the outside wall commemorates Alexander Brodie (d. 1811), Iron Master 'a native of Traquaire [sic], First Inventor of the Register Stoves and Fire Hearths for Ships'. Many notable gravestones from late 17th century onwards.

- Sunday: 10.00am on 2nd and 4th Sunday of the month; as announced for 5th Sunday
- Open by arrangement (01896 830309)

Ⓑ

82 TRAQUAIR HOUSE CHAPEL

**Traquair House
Traquair
EH44 6PW**

Å NT 331 355

⌂ Roman Catholic

⊕ www.traquair.co.uk

The chapel, formerly the billiard room above the brewhouse, replaced the 'secret chapel' in the main house used in penal times. Related memorabilia on view in house, which also contains a priest's hole and secret stairway. The chapel has carved oak panels said to have come from the Chapel of Mary of Guise in Leith, and to be of Flemish origin. The altar is by the Italian sculptor Brumidi.

- Mass 7.00pm, last Thursday, April to October
- Open April 12.00 noon–5.00pm; June, July and August 10.30am–5.00pm; October 11.00am–4.00pm. Access to Chapel is included in admission to grounds (01896 830323)

83   TWEEDSMUIR KIRK

Tweedsmuir
ML12 6QN

NT 101 245

Church of Scotland

www.uppertweeddale.org.uk/
tweedsmuir_kirk_6.html

Linked with Broughton (68),
Drumelzier (69), Skirling (79), Stobo
(80)

13km (8 miles) south of Broughton
on A701

Present building 1874 by John
Lessels to replace earlier church
of 1643. Bell of 1773 still in use.
Major restoration 2002. Oak for the
panelling in the porch is from a tree
planted at Abbotsford by Sir Walter
Scott. The churchyard dates back to
the first church and contains table-
stone graves of the 18th century
and several other stones of interest,
including a Covenanter's grave and
one to the many men who died in the
construction of the Talla reservoir.

- Sunday: 10.00am
- Open daily (01899 880204)

84   ST MUNGO'S CHURCH, WEST LINTON

Chapel Brae
West Linton
EH46 7EP

NT 148 518

Scottish Episcopal

www.stjamespenicuik.co.uk

Linked with St James's Episcopal
Church, Penicuik, Midlothian
(*Sacred Edinburgh and Midlothian*
(89))

A 'Gladstone church' built in 1851,
when it served as both church and
school. Unusually, the church runs
from north to south instead of east to
west. The church is built on a steeply
sloping site. Fine stained glass by C. E.
Kempe.

- Sunday: 11.00am; 2nd Sunday:
  Choral Evensong 5.30pm
- Open by arrangement (01968
  672862)

85 ANCRUM KIRK

Ale and Teviot United Church

**Ancrum
TD8 6UY**

⚐ NT 627 246

⛪ Church of Scotland

🌐 www.aleandteviot.org.uk

Linked with Crailing Kirk (88), Lilliesleaf Kirk (111)

The present church, built of red sandstone, was opened in 1890 to replace an 18th-century building, the remains of which may be seen in the kirkyard, approximately one mile west of the present church. The architects were Hardy & Wight. Stained-glass windows by Ballantine & Son, James Benson and Ballantine & Gardiner.

- Sunday: 10.00am
- Open by arrangement (01835 830318)

86 BEDRULE CHURCH

United Parishes of Ruberslaw

**Bedrule
TD9 8TE**

⚐ NT 599 179

⛪ Church of Scotland

🌐 www.hobkirkruberslaw.org

Linked with Denholm (89), Hobkirk (99), Minto (118), Southdean (126)

By Jedburgh

On an ancient site, the church was rebuilt in 1804 and 1877 and again rebuilt beautifully in 1914 by T. Greenshields Leadbetter as a cruciform church with a tower over the main west entrance. Plaque commemorating Bishop Turnbull, founder of Glasgow University in 1451. Stained glass, including Guild centenary window 1992 and windows by Douglas Strachan 1922. Memorial with interesting link to wartime 'Enigma' decoding project. Fine views over Rule Valley to Ruberslaw.

- Sunday: 9.30am or 11.00am, usually every three weeks; times change every four months: see noticeboard or website for details
- Open by arrangement (01450 860692)

B

87 BOWDEN KIRK

**Bowden
TD6 0SU**

NT 554 301

Church of Scotland

www.melrose-parish.fsnet.co.uk

Linked with Melrose Parish Church (115)

Sitting by St Cuthbert's Way, the pilgrim route from Melrose to Lindisfarne, the church, founded 1128, has a wealth of architectural history. Part of the north wall is possibly 15th century, east end from 1644, cross aisle from 1661, west gable and doorway at west end of north wall 17th century. Repaired 1794. Major alterations 1909 by Peter MacGregor Chalmers. Carved wooden 17th-century laird's loft for Riddell-Carre family. Burial vaults of Riddell-Carre of Cavers-Carre and Dukes of Roxburghe. Memorials, including one to Lady Grizell Baillie, first Deaconess of the Church of Scotland. Many notable tombstones in graveyard.

- Sunday: 9.30am
- Open daily (01896 823339)

88 CRAILING KIRK

Ale and Teviot United Church

**Crailing
TD8 6TL**

NT 682 250

Church of Scotland

www.aleandteviot.org.uk

Linked with Ancrum Kirk (85), Lilliesleaf Kirk (111)

On A698 Jedburgh-to-Kelso road

Built c. 1775 on an ancient site of worship; the bell is dated 1702. The Kirk Session paid for a boat to ferry parishioners from Nisbet on the far side of the River Teviot, the usual fare of one penny being waived on Sunday. Aisle added in the early 19th century, with further alterations and additions 1892. Restoration by Peter MacGregor Chalmers 1907.

- 10.30am on 2nd and 4th Sunday of the month; 6.30pm on 1st Sunday
- Open by arrangement (01835 830318)

89 DENHOLM CHURCH

United Parishes of Ruberslaw

**Denholm
TD9 8NX**

⚐ NT 569 186

⛪ Church of Scotland

⊕ www.hobkirkruberslaw.org

Linked with Bedrule Church (86), Hobkirk Parish Church (99), Minto Church (118), Southdean Parish Church (111)

By Hawick on A698

Dates from 1845 when it was built as the Free Church. A small rectangular church, its interior was much altered in 1957. Wall hangings for 150th anniversary. Situated in a beautiful conservation village which was the birthplace of John Scott, the botanist, and James Murray of the *Oxford English Dictionary*.

- Sunday: 9.30am or 11.00am, usually every three weeks; times change every four months: see notice-board or website for details
- Open by arrangement (01450 860692)

90 EDNAM PARISH CHURCH

**Ednam
TD5 7QL**

⚐ NT 737 372

⛪ Church of Scotland

⊕ www.kelsonorthandednam.org.uk

Linked with Kelso North Parish Church (105)

By Kelso

Built in 1805 by William Elliot as a traditional country kirk. Recast by Hardy & Wight in 1902 when the chancel, porch and vestry were added and the interior was reordered. Situated in the village of Ednam where Henry Francis Lyte, writer of the hymn *Abide with Me*, was born; there is a plaque to Lyte on the bridge over the Eden Water.

- Sunday: 9.30am
- Open July and August, 10.00am–4.00pm or by arrangement (01573 224154)

91 ETTRICK KIRK

**Ettrick
TD7 5HX**

NT 259 145

Church of Scotland

Linked with Kirkhope Kirk, Ettrickbridge (92), Yarrow Kirk (130)

Ettrickhill, 1.5km (1 mile) west of Ettrick village

The present church, built 1824, replaced the post-Reformation Kirk of Ettrick and Rankilburn in which Thomas Boston preached in the early 17th century. Of three lofts, two have separations between the pews to stop the herd's dogs from fighting. The third loft, of the Napier family, has more comfortable seating. Notable features are the pulpit with dove and original ladles for offerings. In the churchyard are the burial plot of the Napier family and the graves of James Hogg 'the Ettrick Shepherd', and Tibbie Shiel.

- Sunday: 11.45am on 3rd Sunday of the month; for 5th Sunday, see local press
- Open daily (01750 82336)

92 KIRKHOPE KIRK, ETTRICKBRIDGE

**Ettrickbridge
TD7 5HW**

NT 390 244

Church of Scotland

Linked with Ettrick Kirk (91), Yarrow Kirk (130)

B7009, 11 km (7 miles) south-west of Selkirk

That it shares the same name as Kirkhope in Upper Ettrick shows its ancient association with Melrose Abbey – yet, in the Middle Ages, any church here belonged to the parish of Yarrow. Of simple rectangular plan, the church features a good stained-glass window and the Buccleuch Aisle of its original patron. Set in a wooded garden beside the steep bank of the Ettrick Linns, there is a lychgate memorial to two world wars.

- 10.00am on 2nd and 4th Sunday of the month; for 5th Sunday, see local press
- Open daily (01750 82336)

93 GALASHIELS OLD PARISH AND ST PAUL'S

**Scott Crescent
Galashiels
TD1 3JU**

⋀ NT 490 362

🏛 Church of Scotland

🌐 www.oldparishandstpauls.org.uk

Built 1878–81 to plans in the Gothic Revival style by George Henderson; main feature is the 58m (190ft) spire. Front porch added 1922. Good glass, including windows by Douglas Strachan, George Henderson, Ballantine & Son and C. E. Kempe. Stone carvings by John Rhind and wood carving by Francis Lynn. 'Father' Willis organ.

- Sunday: 11.00am and 6.30pm
- Open by arrangement (01896 752320)

94 ST PETER'S CHURCH, GALASHIELS

**Abbotsford Road
Galashiels
TD1 3DP**

⋀ NT 496 356

🏛 Scottish Episcopal

0.5km (¼ mile) south of town centre on A7

Attractive Gothic church by John Henderson, 1854, extended by George Henderson, 1881; halls added by Hay & Henderson, 1889. Reredos Sir Robert Lorimer 1914. Stained glass, Memorial brasses. Setting of church with lawns, graveyard, hall and rectory encapsulates the Tractarian ideal. Fine 2-manual tracker organ by Brindley & Foster 1881.

- Sunday: 8.30am and 10.30am
- Open by arrangement (01896 753118)

95 OUR LADY AND ST ANDREW'S, GALASHIELS

**Market Street
Galashiels
TD1 1BY**

A NT 494 362

⛪ Roman Catholic

Linked with High Cross St Cuthbert's, Melrose (117)

The church was built by Robert and Charlotte Hope-Scott of Abbotsford. Gothic Revival building of 1876 designed by William Wardell, a pupil of Pugin, and extended 1866–72 by Goldie & Child. Many interesting features including the late 19th-century decorative scheme, high altar by Earp of London, stone pulpit and font and side altars to Irish and Jesuit saints. The church has had links with the Polish community since 1942 when gifted the Madonna and Child window in the sanctuary.

- Saturday: 6.00pm; Sunday: 11.00am and 1.00pm (Polish/English); Wednesday to Friday: 10.00am; Tuesday: 7.00pm
- Open most days, 9.00am–3.00pm (01896 752328)

 96 ST MARY'S AND OLD PARISH CHURCH, HAWICK

**St Mary's Place
Hawick
TD9 0AN**

A NT 502 144

⛪ Church of Scotland

Close to Heritage Hub in centre of town

There has been a church on this site for 800 years; the present building was constructed in 1764 and reconstructed 1883 after a fire. The tower has a bell-cast roof, clock and weathervane. Inside, the T-plan sanctuary has a fine barrel-vaulted ceiling, a beautiful wooden pulpit incorporating a decorative cross and communion furniture by local craftsmen. The cemetery has a collection of 18th- and 19th-century gravestones.

- Sunday: 11.00am
- Open Wednesday 2.00–4.00pm June to September or by arrangement (01450 378163)

SCOTTISH BORDERS

SELKIRKSHIRE/ ROXBURGHSHIRE

97 ST CUTHBERT'S, HAWICK

**Slitrig Crescent
Hawick
TD9 0EN**

A Sir George Gilbert Scott building of 1858. Reredos by J. Oldrid Scott, 1905. Chancel screen by Robert Lorimer. Some fine stained glass, including contemporary windows of 1995 and 2002.

- Sunday: 9.30am and 10.30am; Wednesday: 11.00am
- Open alternate Mondays 2.00–4.00pm, Wednesday 10.45am–12 noon (01450 370034)

 98 ST MARY'S AND ST DAVID'S, HAWICK

**15 Buccleuch Street
Hawick
TD9 0HH**

NT 499 145

Roman Catholic

Linked with Immaculate Conception, Jedburgh (103), Immaculate Conception, Kelso (107)

The foundation stone was laid in 1843 and the church opened in 1844 with seating for 400. The side chapel was built 1879, increasing the seating to 500. New sacristy late 1960s. Stained-glass window for Father Taggart, 1895. The organ was updated in 1914.

- Saturday: 9.30am; Sunday: 11.30am; Monday, Wednesday, Friday: 10.00am; Thursday: 7.00pm
- Open Saturday 9.00–11.00am (01450 372037)

 (by arrangement)

Note: the NT 501 141 and Scottish Episcopal markers appear under church 97.

99 HOBKIRK PARISH CHURCH

United Parishes of Ruberslaw

Hobkirk
TD9 8JU

A NT 587 109

  Church of Scotland

  www.hobkirkruberslaw.org

Linked with Bedrule Church (86), Denholm Church (89), Minto Church (118), Southdean Parish Church (126)

1.5km (1 mile) west of Bonchester Bridge on A6088

A Christian site for over 900 years. The present Gothic-style church with its massive tower was designed by David Rhind and built in 1863. Stones from the earlier churches are incorporated in the font. The bell is inscribed 'I was made for Hobkirk in 1745'.

- Sunday: 9.45am for four months; then 11.30am for four months; see notice-board for details
- Open by arrangement (01450 860692)

100 HOSELAW CHAPEL

Cheviot Churches

Hoselaw
TD5 8BP

A NT 802 318

  Church of Scotland

  http://cheviotchurches.org

Linked with Hownam Parish Church (101), The Kirk of Yetholm (109), Linton Kirk (112), Morebattle Parish Church (119)

Near Morebattle, by Kelso

Dedicated to the memory of Thomas Leishman, minister of Linton Kirk, and designed 1905 by the architect of the restoration of Linton Kirk, Peter MacGregor Chalmers. Modest but dignified rectangular church with apse. Stained-glass window of Our Lord holding the Sacramental Cup, by S. V. Willis. Fresco in apse of angels holding a banner: 'Alleluia, for the Lord God Omnipotent reigneth'.

- Occasional Evening Communion
- Open during daylight hours (01573 420308)

HOWNAM PARISH CHURCH

Cheviot Churches

**Hownam
TD5 8AL**

 NT 778 193

Church of Scotland

http://cheviotchurches.org

Linked with Hoselaw Chapel (100), The Kirk of Yetholm (109), Linton Kirk (112), Morebattle Parish Church (119)

By Kelso

In an idyllic situation on the haugh by the Kale Water. The original building appears to have been cruciform, but was remodelled in 1752 as a rectangle and substantially modernised in 1844. The interior was refurbished in 1986. From the original church, there remains a round-headed doorway in the south wall, dating from the turn of the 15th and 16th centuries.

- Sunday: 12.30pm on 4th Sunday of the month
- Open daily (01573 420308)

102 **ST JOHN THE EVANGELIST, JEDBURGH**

**The Pleasance
Jedburgh
TD8 6DJ**

NT 651 209

Scottish Episcopal

www.scotland.anglican.org

Significant as the first Oxford Movement church building in Scotland, built in 1844. The designer was John Hayward of Exeter, but it is thought that William Butterfield was responsible for much of the ecclesiologically correct interior. Rood screen of carved oak; the figures added later. Altar, sedilia, pulpit and font in Caen stone, a gift of Queen Adelaide. Original Minton tiles on the floors and chancel walls, with designs after A. W. N. Pugin. The recent removal of the 1937 reredos revealed exquisite altar tiles. Traditionally painted modern icons. Lychgate by Butterfield. Churchyard graves are over a century old.

- Sunday: 9.00am, 10.30am (summer) or 11.00am (winter); see website for other services
- Open 9.00am to dusk (summer), 9.00am–5.00pm (winter) (01835 863892)

103 THE IMMACULATE CONCEPTION (ST MARY'S), JEDBURGH

**2 Old Bongate
Jedburgh
TD8 6DR**

⚲ NT 653 210

⛪ Roman Catholic

Linked with St Mary's and St David's, Hawick (98), Immaculate Conception, Kelso (107)

A good example of architect Reginald Fairlie's simple Catholic churches with attached priest's house. Built in 1937, on the site of a previous building, with an aisleless nave and a semi-octagonal apse; traditional and with good use of materials.

- Saturday: Vigil Mass 5.30pm; details of other services on notice-board
- Open by arrangement (01573 224725)

104 KELSO OLD PARISH CHURCH

**The Butts
Kelso
TD5 7DH**

⚲ NT 729 339

⛪ Church of Scotland

Linked with Sprouston Kirk (127)

Off Market Square, by Knowes car park and adjacent to Kelso Abbey

Octagonal-plan church, James Nisbet, dating from 1773, and altered by William Elliot in 1823. Built to continue worship begun in Kelso Abbey in 1128. Recently extensively restored. Banners of Blues and Royals, presented to the church by the Duke of Roxburghe 1927.

- Sunday: 11.30am
- Open Easter to September, Monday to Friday 10.00am–4.00pm (01573 226254)

105 KELSO NORTH PARISH CHURCH

**Roxburgh Street
Kelso
TD5 7JH**

NT 727 341

Church of Scotland

www.kelsonorthandednam.org.uk

Linked with Ednam Parish Church (90)

Erected 1866 for the congregation of Kelso North Free Church, architect Frederick T. Pilkington. The front of the church is very ornate, designed in the Gothic style, with the tower and spire rising to 55m (180ft). Extensively renovated in 1934 and 1984–9. Although the exterior is quite massive, in contrast the interior is fairly neat and compact.

- Sunday: 11.00am
- Open July and August, Monday to Friday 10.00am–4.00pm or by arrangement (01573 224154)

106 ST ANDREW'S CHURCH, KELSO

**Belmont Place
Kelso
TD5 7JB**

NT 728 337

Scottish Episcopal

http://stmaryandstandrew.org.uk

Linked with St Mary's and All Souls, Coldstream (47)

Opposite Kelso Abbey on B6089

Built 1868 by Sir Robert Rowand Anderson, close to the River Tweed. Anderson also designed the altar, reredos, font and the Robertson family monument sculpted in marble and Caen stone. Decorative wooden chancel roof and decorated pulpit. Stained glass by Henry Holiday, James Powell and Douglas Strachan. Small garden to rear (including Garden Room for meetings and Junior Church).

- Sunday: 8.30am and 10.30am; Thursday: 10.30am
- Open daily 8.00am–4.00pm (01573 224163)

107 THE IMMACULATE CONCEPTION (ST MARY'S), KELSO

**Bowmont Street
Kelso
TD5 7DZ**

⚔ NT 724 344

🏠 Roman Catholic

Linked with St Mary's and St David's, Hawick (98), Immaculate Conception, Jedburgh (103)

Dated 1858, designed by W. W. Wardell of London as a simple 4-bay Gothic church, with chancel added 1935. Stained glass by Hardman and one window by Anne Sinclair, 2003, in memory of Richard Stefani. Altar, reredos and baldacchino of mahogany, designed by Archibald MacPherson 1916, and depicting the Annunciation.

- Sunday: 9.30am; Wednesday: 10.00am
- Open by arrangement (01573 224725)

108 KELSO QUAKER MEETING HOUSE

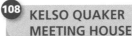

**Abbey Row
Kelso
TD5 7JF**

⚔ NT 729 339

🏠 Quaker

🌐 www.quakerscotland.org/borders

A former coach house adjoining the Old Priory, the Meeting House is a traditional two-storey building of stone and slate, probably dating from before 1800. Collection of eight lino-cut prints of Border views by Earlston artist Tom Davidson. Ministry is welcome in any language, but is most often in English!

- Sunday Meeting for Worship: 10.30am
- Open by arrangement (01835 864445)

SCOTTISH BORDERS

ROXBURGHSHIRE

109 THE KIRK OF YETHOLM, KIRK YETHOLM

Cheviot Churches

Kirk Yetholm
TD5 8PF

NT 826 281

Church of Scotland

http://cheviotchurches.org

Linked with Hoselaw (100), Hownam (101), Linton (112), Morebattle (119)

The church stands on a site in use since David I's apportionment of parishes. Built by Robert Brown 1837 to replace a small dank thatched affair, it is a rectangular-plan Gothic church of local whinstone with cream sandstone dressings. The interior has a lightness belied by the sombre exterior. Stained glass by Ballantine & Son, Edinburgh. The medieval bell is still in use. As the nearest burial ground to Flodden, the graveyard is believed to contain officers who fell in that battle (1513). Gravestones 17th century.

- Sunday: 10.00am
- Open during daylight hours (01573 420308)

110 MANOR KIRK, KIRKTON MANOR

Kirkton Manor
EH45 9JH

NT 220 380

Church of Scotland

Linked with Lyne Kirk (74)

By Peebles

First referred to in 1186 as 'the Chapel of Maineure'. Tradition speaks of an earlier chapel of the 4th century dedicated to St Gordian, a martyred Roman soldier. The present building was completed in 1874. The bell, rung before every service, is inscribed 'In honore Santi Gordiani MCCCCLXXVIII' and is one of the oldest bells in use in Scotland. Pewter baptismal basin, inscribed 'Manner Kirk 1703'. The pipe organ, originally built by Peter Conacher in 1889, came from Pencaitland Church and was rebuilt in Manor Kirk in October 2002.

- Sunday: 11.00am on 2nd, 3rd and 4th Sunday of each month, 6.30pm on 5th Sunday
- Open daily (01721 721749)

111 LILLIESLEAF KIRK

Ale and Teviot United Church

Lilliesleaf
TD6 9JD

⚔ NT 539 253
⛪ Church of Scotland
🌐 www.aleandteviot.org.uk

Linked with Ancrum Kirk (85), Crailing Kirk (88)

East of Lilliesleaf village

The church of 1771 was extended in 1883 and transformed by the addition of the west part of the nave and bell-tower in 1910. Good stained glass by William Wilson, 1966. Medieval font and ancient child's stone coffin.

- Sunday: 11.30am
- Open daily (01835 830318)

112 LINTON KIRK

Cheviot Churches

Linton
TD5 8AE

⚔ NT 773 262
⛪ Church of Scotland
🌐 http://cheviotchurches.org

Linked with Hoselaw (100), Hownam (101), Yetholm (109), Morebattle (119)

On B6436, 1.5km (1 mile) north of Morebattle

On a sandy knoll, a 12th-century church much altered in 1616, 1774 and 1813, and finally restored in 1912 by Peter MacGregor Chalmers. It retains its Norman feel; a Norman font and chancel stalls are of particular interest. The Norman stone above the porch is said to depict a knight on horseback lancing two creatures. The Leishman father-and-son ministries completed most of the present improvements.

- 11.15am on 1st Sunday of the month; Tuesday: 6.30pm
- Open during daylight hours (01573 420308)

113 MAKERSTOUN CHURCH

Kelso Country Churches
Makerstoun
TD5 7PA

Ⓐ NT 669 331

Ⓗ Church of Scotland

Linked with Roxburgh Parish Church (123), Smailholm Church (125), Stichill Parish Church (129)

800 metres (½ mile) north of Makerstoun village, 6.5km (4 miles) north-west of Kelso

Built 1808; bell-tower on south wall, recently repaired, has '1808' inscribed on it. The church is light with plain glass windows and original pine pews, pulpit and precentor's desk. Gallery and Sunday School upstairs. The setting of the church and churchyard is beautiful and peaceful.

- 10.00am on 2nd and 4th Sunday of the month
- Open by arrangement (01573 470607)

114 MAXTON PARISH CHURCH

Maxton
TD6 0RN

Ⓐ NT 610 303

Ⓗ Church of Scotland

⊕ www.maxton.bordernet.co.uk/church.html

Linked with Mertoun Parish Church (62), Newtown Church (121), St Boswells Parish Church (128)

On the north-west edge of Maxton village

On St Cuthbert's Way and dedicated to St Cuthbert. Reputed to have been a place of worship on this site for almost 1,000 years. Originally oblong, thatched until 1790. North aisle added 1866, vestry 1962. Wyvern organ. Stained glass by J. H. Corham gifted 1914; Hebrew and Latin inscriptions; Maxton War Memorial within church. Burgerhuys bell 1609. Burial vault of Kers of Littledean.

- 11.45am on 2nd and 4th Sunday of the month; 5th Sunday: service in rotation with Mertoun, Newtown and St Boswells
- Open by arrangement (01361 882728)

115 MELROSE PARISH CHURCH

St Cuthbert's

**Weirhill
Melrose
TD6 9LJ**

⚑ NT 543 344

⛪ Church of Scotland

🌐 www.melrose-parish.fsnet.co.uk

Linked with Bowden Kirk (87)

The 4-stage tower and octagonal spire is all that remains of the 1808 church by John Smith, damaged by fire in 1908. The reconstructed church was designed in a matching classical style by J. M. Dick Peddie in 1911. Interior is spacious with tall Doric columns supporting the vaulted roof. Mahogany panelling in the chancel decorated with carved flowers and fruit. Stained glass by Christopher Whall.

- Sunday: 11.00am
- Open Monday, Wednesday and Friday 9.00am–1.00pm (01896 823339)

116 HOLY TRINITY, MELROSE

**20 High Cross Avenue
Melrose
TD6 9SU**

⚑ NT 540 342

⛪ Scottish Episcopal

🌐 www.holytrinitymelrose.org.uk

On road to Darnick

Built in the Early English style by Benjamin Ferrey 1846–50. Decorated chancel and transepts by Hay & Henderson 1900. The chancel floor is mosaic. Open timber roof carried on mask corbels. Stained-glass windows in transept 1900 by Kempe; other commemorative glass by Mayer & Co. and W. Wilson 1963.

- Sunday: 8.30am and 11.00am; 6.30pm on 1st Sunday of the month
- Open by arrangement (01896 822626)

117 HIGH CROSS ST CUTHBERT'S, MELROSE

**High Cross Avenue
Melrose
TD6 9SQ**

NT 541 342

Roman Catholic

Linked with Our Lady and St Andrew's, Galashiels (95)

Opposite Holy Trinity Episcopal Church

Built as the United Presbyterian Church in 1867, the church has been Catholic since 1985. Romanesque Revival in style designed by Peddie & Kinnear, the church has a gabled front and an arcade with red and yellow voussoirs. The 3-stage tower with its octagonal spire was added in 1872. Simple interior. Pipe organ. Attractive stained-glass window depicting Jesus blessing children. Part of Melrose Town Trail. 25th-anniversary celebrations in 2010.

- Sunday: 9.15am, Holy Days of Obligation 6.30pm
- Open most days, 10.00am–dusk (6.00pm in summer) (01896 752328)

118 MINTO CHURCH

United Parishes of Ruberslaw

**Minto
TD9 8SG**

NT 567 201

Church of Scotland

www.hobkirkruberslaw.org

Linked with Bedrule Church (86), Denholm Church (89), Hobkirk Parish Church (99), Southdean Parish Church (126)

By Hawick

Designed by William Playfair, the church dates from 1830, the interior recast in 1934. In a Gothic style with a square tower. Fine external war memorial. Panoramic views of Teviotdale and Minto Hill.

- Sunday: 9.30am or 11.00am, usually every three weeks; times change every four months: see notice-board or website for details
- Open by arrangement (01450 860692)

119 MOREBATTLE PARISH CHURCH

Cheviot Churches

**Morebattle
TD5 9QR**

NT 772 250

Church of Scotland

http://cheviotchurches.org

Linked with Hoselaw Chapel (100), Hownam Parish Church (101), The Kirk of Yetholm (109), Linton Kirk (112)

By Kelso

The church of 'Mereboda' is recorded as belonging to the Diocese of Glasgow from about 1116. The building was burned down in 1544 and rebuilt; the present structure dates substantially from 1757, extensions having been made in 1899 and 1903. It is oblong in plan, with chancel, porch and vestry which seem to be additions. Look for the plan in the porch which shows the archaeological work carried out in the early 1900s, and inscriptions painted on fabric on the west wall.

- Sunday: 11.15am except 1st Sunday of the month
- Open during daylight hours (01573 420308)

 **120 NEWCASTLETON CHURCH**

**Montague Street
Newcastleton
TD9 0QZ**

NY 482 877

Church of Scotland

Linked with Saughtree Kirk (124)

A bright and welcoming building dating from 1888 but with a more modern feel. Memorial to George Armstrong, founder of the world's first children's hospital. Millennium stained-glass window by Alex Haynes of Brampton.

- Sunday: 10.00am and 6.00pm
- Open Wednesday 10.00–11.30am or by arrangement (01228 560866)

SCOTTISH BORDERS

ROXBURGHSHIRE

121 NEWTOWN CHURCH

**St Boswells Road
Newtown St Boswells
TD6 0PQ**

NT 315 693

Church of Scotland

Linked with Mertoun Parish Church
(62), Maxton Parish Church (114),
St Boswells Parish Church (128)

Church opened in 1868, designed
by John Paterson. Built in pink
sandstone with cream stone margins;
the simple nave and aisles change to a
many-sided apse flanked by porches,
one with a pyramid roof, the other
with a spire. Contains memorials to
past ministers.

- 9.30am on 1st, 2nd and 3rd Sunday
  of the month, 5.00pm on 4th
  Sunday; 5th Sunday: service in
  rotation with Maxton, Mertoun and
  St Boswells
- Open by arrangement (01835
  823457)

122 OXNAM KIRK

**Oxnam
TD8 6RD**

NT 701 190

Church of Scotland

www.oxnamkirk.co.uk

Off A68, by Jedburgh

On the site of a medieval church
dating from before 1153. A
characteristic Scottish 18th-century
church with plain glass and
whitewashed walls, the present
church was built in 1738 and enlarged
to form a T-plan in 1874. Many fine
17th- and 18th-century gravestones.
Continuo pipe organ by Lammermuir
Pipe Organs 1990.

- 10.30am on 1st, 3rd and 5th Sunday
  of the month
- Open by arrangement (01573 440761)

B

123 ROXBURGH PARISH CHURCH

Kelso Country Churches

Roxburgh
TD5 8LZ

⚔ NT 700 307

 Church of Scotland

Linked with Makerstoun Church (113), Smailholm Church (125), Stichill Parish Church (129)

4km (2½ miles) west of Kelso on A699

Built 1752, repaired 1828, with additions (including the north aisle) 1878. Fine painted heraldic panels. Stained glass 1947 by W. Wilson. The exterior has a pair of cubic sundials. In the graveyard is the (roofless) burial vault of the Kers of Chatto. Fine modern continuo pipe organ, Lammermuir Pipe Organs 1990.

- 11.30am on 2nd and 4th Sunday of the month
- Open by arrangement (01573 470607)

124 SAUGHTREE KIRK

Saughtree
TD9 0SW

⚔ NY 562 968

 Church of Scotland

Linked with Newcastleton Church (120)

14.5km (9 miles) north of Newcastleton on B6357

A simple country kirk dating from 1872 enjoying views to the English Border. Fine patterned coloured-glass window. Interesting embroidered pulpit fall depicting the Trinity.

- Sunday: 9.30am on 2nd Sunday, and occasional evening services
- Open by arrangement (01228 560866)

125 ## SMAILHOLM CHURCH

**Smailholm
TD5 7RT**

NT 649 364

Church of Scotland

Linked with Makerstoun Church
(113), Roxburgh Parish Church
(123), Stichill Parish Church (129)

Built 1630s on 12th-century
foundations, altered 1820s and the
interior reordered during the 20th
century. The east window, depicting
St Cuthbert and St Giles, was erected
in memory of Sir Walter Scott, whose
family farmed at Sandyknowes by
Smailholm Tower. Birdcage belfry
with external bell-rope and outside
stairs to the laird's loft.

- 10.00am on 1st and 3rd Sunday of
  the month
- Open by arrangement (01573
  470607)

---

126 ## SOUTHDEAN PARISH CHURCH

**United Parishes of
Ruberslaw**

**Southdean
TD9 8TW**

NT 624 109

Church of Scotland

www.hobkirkruberslaw.org

Linked with Bedrule (86), Denholm
(89), Hobkirk (99), Minto (118)

1.5km (1 mile) south of Chesters on
A6088

Designed by George Grant of Glasgow;
built 1876 near two ruined churches
of 12th and 17th centuries. Font,
12th century. Super-altar set into
communion table, one of only two
known in Scotland. Good stained glass.
Memorial to James Thomson (1700–48),
author of *Rule Britannia* and *The Seasons*,
whose father was parish minister.
Before the Battle of Otterburn 1388, the
Earl of Douglas and his army met at the
12th-century church, where the dead
were later buried.

- Special services only
- Open by arrangement (01450 860692)

127 SPROUSTON KIRK

**Sprouston
TD5 8HJ**

NT 757 353

Church of Scotland

Linked with Kelso Old Parish Church (104)

3km (2 miles) east of Kelso on B6350

There has been a church in Sprouston since the 17th century. The present building was built in 1781, though the bellcote bears the date 1703 and a 12th-century piscina is built into the chancel. The minister in 1911 won 1st and 3rd prizes out of 36,000 entries in the *Daily Mail* National Sweet Pea Competition, enabling the new chancel to be built with the £1,500 prize money. Douglas Strachan window of *The Fall of Lucifer*. Pulpit falls of sweet peas embroidered by Mrs Doreen West.

- Sunday: 10.00am
- Open by arrangement (01573 226254)

128 ST BOSWELLS PARISH CHURCH

**St Boswells
TD6 0BB**

NT 594 310

Church of Scotland

Linked with Mertoun Parish Church (62), Maxton Parish Church (114), Newtown Church (121)

South side of St Boswells main street near village hall

Built 1844 as the Free Church, originally square with an earth floor. Wooden floor and seating added later in 19th century. Became United Free Church in 1900, St Modan's Church of Scotland in 1929, and St Boswells Parish Church in 1952 when the old church at Benrig was abandoned. Substantially renovated and chancel added 1957–9. Pipe organ. Stained glass in chancel by McLundie and in east gable by Liz Rowley.

- Sunday: 10.30am; 5th Sunday: service in rotation with Maxton, Mertoun and Newtown
- Open by arrangement (01835 822425)

129 STICHILL PARISH CHURCH

Stichill
TD5 7TA

NT 711 383

Church of Scotland

Linked with Makerstoun Church (113), Roxburgh Parish Church (123), Smailholm Church (125)

West end of Stichill village, 5km (3 miles) north of Kelso

This is the second (or third) church on the site, built around the 1780s. It has an outside stairway to the laird's loft, and a burial aisle to the Pringle family on the east gable. The interior is light, with stained glass only in the chancel. Adjoining the church is a stable, altered in 2003 to a small church hall, kitchen and toilet.

- Sunday: 11.15am
- Open by arrangement (01573 470607)

130 YARROW KIRK

Yarrow
TD7 5LA

NT 358 278

Church of Scotland

Linked with Ettrick Kirk (91), Kirkhope Kirk, Ettrickbridge (92)

On A708, 13km (8 miles) west of Selkirk

The present church, built in 1640, replaced the historic 'St Mary's of the Lowes' or 'The Forest Kirk', dating from the 12th century, on the hillside above St Mary's Loch. Sir Walter Scott and James Hogg, 'the Ettrick Shepherd', were regular worshippers. With a traditional T-plan, it was considerably adapted and improved over the years. It was gutted by fire in 1922 but restored. Memorial windows by Douglas Strachan. Sundial on corner of building.

- 10.00am on 1st and 3rd Sunday of the month; for 5th Sunday, see local press
- Open daily (01750 82336)

Index

References are to each church's entry number in the gazetteer.